Drought Management Policies and Economic Effects in Urban Areas of California, 1987–1992

Lloyd S. Dixon

Nancy Y. Moore

Ellen M. Pint

Supported by the
California Urban Water Agencies
California Department of Water Resources
National Science Foundation

RAND

PREFACE

This report presents results from a set of interrelated projects at RAND on the impacts of the 1987-1992 drought on urban and agricultural users. It contains a conceptual discussion of the definition and measurement of the effects of drought in urban areas, an analysis of data collected from 85 urban water agencies on drought management strategies and customer responses during the drought, and an analysis of household water demand and consumer surplus losses due to the drought in Alameda County Water District. The purpose of this work is to provide the conceptual framework and background information needed to value the drought's effect on residential, commercial, and industrial users. It should be of interest to legislators, water managers, researchers, and members of the general public who are concerned about the cost of urban water shortages and the development of water policies that are efficient, equitable, and environmentally sound.

Analyses of other aspects of the 1987-1992 drought can be found in

- *California's 1991 Drought Water Bank: Economic Impacts in the Selling Regions*, Lloyd S. Dixon, Nancy Y. Moore, and Susan W. Schechter, RAND, MR-301-CDWR/RC, 1993
- *Assessment of the Economic Impacts of California's Drought on Urban Areas: A Research Agenda*, Nancy Y. Moore, Ellen M. Pint, and Lloyd S. Dixon, RAND, MR-251-CUWA/RC, 1993
- *The Impact of Water Supply Reductions on San Joaquin Valley Agriculture*, Lloyd S. Dixon and Larry L. Dale, RAND, DRU-892-EPA, 1994.

The analysis presented here was funded by California Urban Water Agencies (CUWA), an association of 11 large wholesale and retail water agencies; California's Department of Water Resources; and the National Science Foundation.

CONTENTS

FIGURES

TABLES

SUMMARY

During the 1987-1992 California drought, urban water agencies were frequently unable to meet the existing consumption patterns of their customers. They developed policies for resolving the imbalance between supply and demand that included

- quantity restrictions limiting the amount of water a household could buy in a given period, often accompanied by price surcharges for use above the limit

- type-of-use restrictions, such as prohibitions on washing off driveways and sidewalks or irrigating residential lots during the day

- public education programs, including bill inserts; television, radio, and newspaper announcements; school programs; and public displays

- device distribution programs, involving low-flow shower heads, toilet dams, toilet leak detectors, or rebates for installing ultra-low-flush toilets

- price increases, which can take the form of higher prices for all levels of water use, or increasing block rate structures

- supply augmentation strategies, including increased ground water pumping, greater use of reclaimed water, and water transfers through the state-run Drought Water Bank in 1991.

This report presents the results of two related studies that assess the economic effects of these drought management policies on urban areas. The first study, a survey of urban water agencies, provides information on agencies' drought management policies and the response of various customer classes in terms of reduced water use. The second study estimates welfare losses for residential customers in Alameda County Water District, which implemented a sharply increasing block rate price structure as one of its drought management policies. These studies can help inform legislators, water managers, researchers, and the general public about the cost of urban water shortages and help in formulating water policies that are efficient, equitable, and environmentally sound.

VALUING DROUGHT EFFECTS

Valuing the effects of water supply cutbacks in urban areas requires a solid conceptual framework for measuring changes in well-being. We adopt a concept that is commonly used in the economics literature to value changes in well-being due to various policy changes: willingness-to-pay. In the context of the drought, willingness-to-pay is defined as the maximum individuals would have been willing to pay to avoid the drought management strategies imposed by water agencies. We discuss how various drought management policies generate willingness-to-pay among residential users. We then discuss the effects of water supply reductions on business firms and how these effects translate into willingness-to-pay, first by individuals who receive firm profits and then by individuals who receive wages and salaries from the firm. We conclude this discussion of a framework for valuing the effects of drought by examining two approaches that quantify willingness-to-pay.

IDENTIFYING EFFECTS OF WATER SUPPLY REDUCTIONS

The first step in valuing the impact of water supply cutbacks in urban areas is to understand which drought management policies were adopted, what types of water users were affected, and what changes in water use resulted. To provide a better understanding of these issues, we conducted a survey of 85 urban water agencies scattered throughout California in 1993. The survey collected data on drought management strategies and consumer responses for the years between 1986 and 1991. We focused on this period because 1986 was the last normal water year before the drought began, and 1991 was the last year for which data were available at the time of the survey.

In our analysis of the survey responses, we discuss the changes in water use during the drought that were reported by participating agencies. Analyses were conducted by customer classes (residential, commercial, industrial, public authority, agricultural, and other), regions of the state (San Francisco Bay Area, Southern California, and the rest of the state), and size of population served (10,000-50,000,

50,001-100,000, and over 100,000). We then discuss the drought management policies adopted by the agencies and provide a qualitative sense of which policies caused the largest losses among users and which types of users were most affected.

Changes in Water Use

Based on our survey results, the bulk of the drought's effects occurred in 1991. Overall, water use in our sample was fairly stable between 1986 and 1990 but dropped significantly in 1991. The population of California grew steadily during this period; the result was a 5 percent drop in per capita water use between 1986 and 1990, and a further 14 percent drop in 1991.

Changes in water use varied across the state. Per capita water use fell by a total of nearly 20 percent in the San Francisco Bay Area from 1987 to 1989, and then dropped another 12 percent in 1991. In contrast, per capita water use in Southern California changed little between 1986 and 1990, but dropped 16 percent in 1991.

Table S.1 shows the decline in water use between 1990 and 1991 by customer class for the entire state. Because all customer classes exhibit sizable declines, it suggests that each class should be examined in assessing the effects of the drought. In terms of the aggregate effect of drought management policies, however, the impacts on residential and commercial classes are probably most important because these two customer groups account for approximately 85 percent of the water use in our sample.

We are unable to disentangle the effect of the drought from other confounding factors, such as the economic recession that affected California in 1990-1991, changes in industrial wastewater discharge standards, and the threat of litigation for water pollution. It appears highly likely, however, that the decreased use by residential and public authority/institutional customers was largely due to drought management policies. There is more uncertainty in how much of the commercial, industrial, and agricultural reductions were due to the drought, but it seems likely that drought management policies were a primary factor.

Table S.1

Percentage Change in Water Use Between 1990 and 1991, by Customer Class

Customer Class	Percentage Change
Total Water Use	-12.4
Residential	-14.1
Single-Dwelling Unit	-19.3
Multiple-Dwelling Unit	-12.2
Commercial	-11.1
Industrial	-15.6
Public Authority/Institutional	-23.0
Agricultural[a]	-24.8

[a]Increased groundwater pumping may have partially offset this decline in agency deliveries.

Drought Management Strategies

The magnitude of economic losses can be influenced by the types of drought management policies used by water agencies to induce changes in water use.[1] We found that a sizable proportion of agencies adopted quantity and type-of-use restrictions, public education and device distribution programs, price-structure changes, and supply augmentation strategies.

Our investigation of drought management strategies suggests the following:

- Mandatory quantity restrictions coupled with price surcharges for excess use were common. The quantity restrictions were widely violated by residential users. However, commercial and industrial users apparently were shielded from adverse impacts to some extent.

- Type-of-use restrictions were common but not well-enforced.

- Public education and device distribution programs were widespread and focused on residential users. These programs presumably reduced willingness-to-pay to avoid drought management policies by facilitating conservation efforts.

---

[1]For example, allowing customers to choose which uses to cut, or to pay extra to continue high-valued uses, may result in smaller economic losses for a given level of cutbacks.

- Average water cost increased for all customer classes during the drought, which clearly had negative effects on consumers. The increases were comparable for residential, commercial, and industrial users, but lower for agricultural users.

- More than half of the urban water agencies responding to the survey received supplies from the 1991 Drought Water Bank. These purchases amounted to approximately 10 percent of 1991 usage by these agencies and suggest that the water bank generated sizable urban benefits.

VALUING RESIDENTIAL LOSSES DURING THE DROUGHT

To estimate the relationship between water use and water prices for residential customers in single-dwelling units, we use water billing information, tax assessor records, and weather data for Alameda County Water District (ACWD), which is located in the southeast San Francisco Bay area. ACWD was chosen because it implemented a steeply increasing block rate structure as one of its drought management policies during 1991 and 1992, and it was able to provide an unusually comprehensive data set covering 600 households over a 10-year period from 1982 to 1992. Although the price structure allows us to measure customer responses to dramatic water price changes, it also creates difficulties in estimating these responses because only high water users pay high prices. This conflicts with the normal economic response of reduced consumption when prices are high.

As a result of the correlation between high prices and high use, the ordinary least squares approach to estimating a statistical relationship between price and quantity consumed results in upward-sloping demand at high prices. We explored the use of fixed effects models, which allow each household to have its own constant term in the regression equation, but these also resulted in upward-sloping demand at high prices. The most successful technique proved to be a computationally intensive maximum likelihood approach, which modeled the households' responses to the block rate structure. These demand relationships were then used as an estimate of households' willingness-to-pay to avoid cutbacks in water use. We found average welfare losses per household from July 1991 to December 1992 in the range of $14-$23 per household, or a total of $750,000 to $1,270,000 for the 54,000 households in the ACWD tax assessor records. However, because of the complexity of the models, we were not able to control for other drought management policies, such as public education, device distribution, and type-of-use restrictions, which may cause us to overestimate or underestimate welfare losses.

CONCLUSION

By 1991, the drought was having widespread effects on water use in all sectors. Our findings suggest that the largest effects occurred in the residential sector, which suffered nearly a 20 percent cutback in 1991 water use per capita relative to 1986. Given that residential use accounts for approximately two-thirds of overall urban water use, this suggests that future studies to quantify aggregate drought effects should focus on the residential sector. A pilot study of the economic impacts of the drought on households living in single-dwelling units in Alameda County Water District found average losses per household in the range of $14-$23 as a result of water price increases over the period from July 1991 to December 1992.

Water use also declined substantially in the commercial and industrial sectors (15 percent and 20 percent, respectively, between 1986 and 1991). This is somewhat surprising, because the survey responses suggest that these sectors were shielded to a large extent from drought management policies, but the large declines were probably due in part to factors other than the drought. The economic recession that affected California in 1990-1991 most likely had an important effect on water use and economic activity. The drought was probably the overriding factor explaining reduction in residential water use, but the importance of the drought relative to other factors is less clear for the commercial and industrial sectors. The shielding of commercial and industrial users from drought management policies suggests that wages, salaries, and profits on the whole were not substantially affected by the drought, although there were probably certain subsectors, such as the landscaping industry, in which the effects were significant.[2] The large declines in water use relative to wages and salaries also suggest that the commercial and industrial sectors were able to make at least some reductions in water use without substantial cuts in wages, salaries, and profits, but further evidence is needed to verify this hypothesis.

Finally, the 1991 Drought Water Bank was an important source of water to many urban agencies. A majority of those receiving water had no alternate sources, which suggests that drought effects would have been considerably worse without the water bank.

---

[2]Note that depressed activity during the drought may possibly be compensated by greater activity than normal after the drought.

ACKNOWLEDGMENTS

The analysis presented here would not have been possible without the information provided by 85 urban water agencies spread throughout California. Agency staff donated considerable time to fill out a lengthy and detailed questionnaire on drought management practices and water use. The agencies responding to our survey are listed in Appendix B, and we thank them wholeheartedly for their efforts.

We would also like to thank the Project Advisory Committee for help in defining the project, designing the survey, and encouraging agencies to fill out the survey. The committee was headed by Lyle Hoag, executive director of California Urban Water Agencies (CUWA). Committee members were Art Bruington of Municipal Water District of Orange County, Leo Cournoyer of Santa Clara Valley Water District, Greg Ford of East Bay Municipal Utility District, Bob Harding and Tim Quinn of Metropolitan Water District, Ray Hoagland and Steve McCaulay of the California Department of Water Resources, Chris Marioka of San Francisco Water Department, Paul Piraino of Alameda County Water District, James Van Haun of Orange County Water District, and Richard West of Los Angeles Department of Water and Power.

Paul Piraino and Leasa Cleland at the Alameda County Water District graciously provided access to water billing and tax assessor data originally collected for a water demand study conducted by Brown and Caldwell. They also assisted in interpreting the data and providing comments on a draft version of our water demand analysis.

Several people provided helpful comments on an initial draft of this report. We would like to thank Rosalie Bock, David Fullerton, Lyle Hoag, Ray Hoagland, and Wendy Illingsworth for their input. We also thank Elizabeth Sloss and Glenn Gotz of RAND for their insightful reviews, which greatly improved the presentation of our findings.

Theo Downes-Le Guin, Melissa Bradley, Jo Levy, and Beverly Weidmer of RAND's Survey Research Group provided valuable assistance in designing and fielding the survey and coding the survey responses. We thank them for their conscientious work. John Adams also provided useful advice on survey sampling techniques. Robert Young and Janet Hanley provided computer programming assistance. Pat Williams helped with typing and correcting the document, and Christina Pitcher skillfully edited the document and shepherded it through the publications process.

Finally, we thank California Urban Water Agencies, the California Department of Water Resources, and the National Science Foundation for their financial support.

Any opinions, findings, and conclusions or recommendations expressed in this material are those of the authors and do not necessarily reflect the views of the National Science Foundation.

1. INTRODUCTION

Continued population growth and regulatory requirements for increased in-stream water flows to protect fish and wildlife are stressing the ability of California's current water supply infrastructure to meet water demands at current water prices and increasing the likelihood of water shortages. Projections of future water supply and demand (including environmental uses) indicate that the gap between supply and demand will widen to 4.1 million acre-feet in average water years and 7.4 million acre-feet in drought years by 2020. (See Figure 1.1.) Additional conservation and supply augmentation might narrow the gap by 1.4-3.0 million acre-feet in average years and by 3.2-5.5 million acre-feet in drought years, but additional environmental requirements (based on Endangered Species Act biological opinions and Environmental Protection Agency [EPA] Bay-Delta standards) could widen the gap by 1.0-3.0 million acre-feet.[1] Therefore, if California's economy and environment are to remain healthy, an issue of central importance is the proper allocation of the state's limited water supplies across many competing uses.

The 1987-1992 California drought, combined with earlier increases in in-stream water requirements, caused severe water supply shortages. An assessment of the economic impacts of these water supply shortages on the state's environment, residents, and businesses can help inform legislators, water managers, and the general public about the cost of water shortages to various sectors. A better understanding of the effects of these shortages will likely help in formulating water policies that are more efficient, equitable, and environmentally sound. In particular, it should enter into decisions about how to allocate water among competing uses and whether to invest in new water projects.

The focus of this report is the impact of water supply shortages on urban areas. We take advantage of the shortages in urban areas during the drought to examine these effects empirically. In an earlier report,

---

[1]See California Department of Water Resources [1994], pp. 12-13.

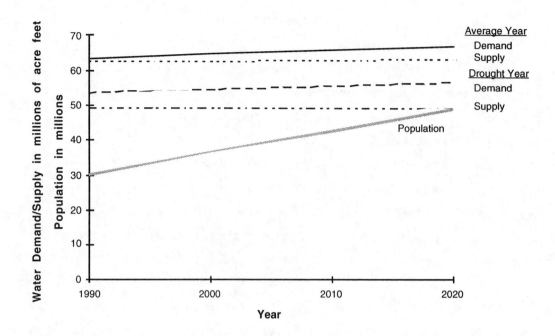

SOURCE: California Department of Water Resources [1994].

Figure 1.1--Projected Water Demand and Supply in California

we evaluated existing studies of the urban impacts of the California drought and outlined a number of approaches for valuing the effect of the drought on urban users.[2] Our literature review found reports that focused on a particular year, a particular class of customers, or a particular location, but we did not find a comprehensive, statewide study of the costs of water shortages to urban users.

Key studies we reviewed included *Cost of Industrial Water Shortages* (Wade, Hewitt, and Nussbaum [1991]), which valued willingness-to-pay for water based on the cost per acre-foot of conservation projects in 22 industrial categories using 1990 data; *Commercial and Industrial Water Use in Southern California* (Dziegielewski, Rodrigo, and Opitz [1990]), which estimated average water use per employee for various commercial and industrial sectors; *The Costs of Water Shortages: Case Study of Santa Barbara* (Spectrum Economics, Inc., and Sycamore Associates [1991]), which showed how residential water consumption and billing changed in response to drought management policies and estimated the

---

[2]See Moore, Pint, and Dixon [1993].

value of dead and damaged landscaping in 1990; and *The Societal and Environmental Costs of the Continuing California Drought* (Gleick and Nash [1991]), which collected information on the statewide effects of the drought but did not attempt to place a dollar value on those effects. Although these studies provided useful information, there were many gaps in the available data that, without additional research, precluded estimation of the dollar value of economic losses due to the drought.

A preliminary survey of California Urban Water Agencies (CUWA) members also revealed that the extent of water supply shortages, types of drought management policies, target cutbacks by customer class, and actual water use by customer class varied substantially among agencies. Thus, it could be very misleading to try to determine the economic effects of the drought throughout California's urban areas by extrapolating from the experience of a few water agencies. We concluded that the first step in quantifying urban drought effects--before we could even determine which approach or combination of approaches to valuing the effects made sense--should be a survey of urban water agencies to collect the necessary information.

Thus, one of the two related research projects described in this report is an analysis of data from a survey of urban retail water agencies, throughout the state, on drought management policies and consumer response between 1986 and 1991. We focused on this period because 1986 was the last normal water year before the drought began, and 1991 was the last year for which data were available when the survey was fielded. Although the drought continued into 1992, its effects were probably greatest in 1991.[3]

The second research project described in this report takes the extra step of estimating the dollar value of drought-related losses to residential households served by a particular agency. We conducted a pilot study of welfare losses due to water price increases during the

---

[3]Precipitation and the Sacramento River Index indicated an easing of the drought in 1992, although runoff and reservoir storage remained low. See Dziegielewski, Garbharran, and Langowski [1993], p. 71.

drought for households living in single-dwelling units[4] in the Alameda County Water District (ACWD), located in the southeast San Francisco Bay Area. We were able to make use of an unusually detailed data set covering bimonthly household water use at 600 single-dwelling units from 1982 to 1992, collected from archived records for a water demand forecast conducted by Brown and Caldwell Consultants [1992]. This data set allowed us to estimate customer responses to an increasing block rate structure implemented by ACWD during 1991 and 1992, and the resulting welfare losses over the same period.

The report is organized as follows. Section 2 provides background information on the severity of the drought and outlines our conceptual framework for measuring drought effects. We describe our survey data collection efforts and examine changes in water use during the drought in Section 3. In Section 4, we characterize water agencies' drought management strategies and investigate the effects of the 1991 Drought Water Bank on urban areas. Section 5 describes our pilot study of residential welfare losses due to the drought, including estimation of the underlying relationship between water use and water prices. We summarize our findings and recommend appropriate areas for further research to more accurately estimate the drought's effects on urban water customers in Section 6. The survey instrument is included as Appendix A. Listings of the water agencies that participated in the survey and that received 1991 Drought Water Bank water follow in Appendixes B and C, respectively. Appendix D provides technical details regarding the models used to estimate the water demand relationship for Alameda County Water District.

---

[4]Single-dwelling units are defined as housing units where one water meter serves one dwelling unit. They are distinct from multiple-dwelling units (such as apartment buildings and condominiums) where one water meter serves many dwelling units.

2. BACKGROUND AND CONCEPTUAL FRAMEWORK

This section provides background information on the 1987-1992 California drought and describes a conceptual framework for evaluating its economic effects on urban areas. We first describe the severity of water supply shortages between 1987 and 1992. We then outline the process through which water supply shortages are translated into effects on urban users and then discuss how these effects might be valued.

WATER SUPPLY SHORTAGES BETWEEN 1987 AND 1992

Between 1987 and 1992, annual statewide precipitation was about three-quarters of its recorded historical average, while runoff was only one-half of average.[1] Figure 2.1 shows the drought's cumulative effect on average statewide precipitation and runoff. Whereas the cumulative statewide deficit in precipitation was less than one and a half years' worth of rain, the cumulative statewide runoff deficit was three years' worth.[2]

Water shortages were not evenly distributed across California. Figure 2.2 shows how the cumulative statewide precipitation and runoff deficits from 1987 to 1992 were distributed among hydrologic regions. Because most regions of California have access to several sources of supply--local surface water, ground water, and imported water-- hydrologic data alone are insufficient to determine the impact of the drought on water use. Note, however, that the cumulative deficit was the highest--over four years of normal runoff--in the Central Coast region (ranging from Santa Barbara to north of Monterey), which has little capability to import water from other regions.

_____

[1]_Precipitation_ includes water that evaporates or is absorbed by vegetation; _runoff_ represents water that can be captured by the state's reservoir system and used by its population.

[2]Water years (running from October 1 to September 30) are classified as "wet," "above normal," "below normal," "dry," and "critical" based on annual precipitation, runoff, and reservoir storage relative to the average. On this basis, 1987-88 and 1990-92 were classified as critical, and 1989 as dry.

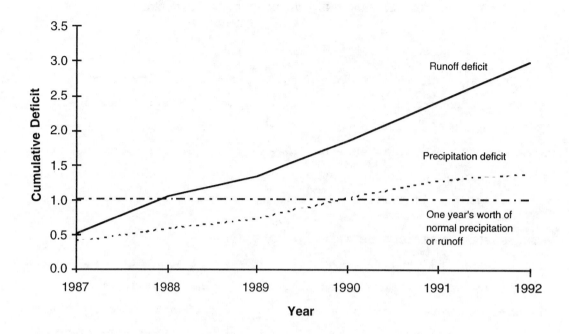

SOURCE: California Department of Water Resources [1991] and Dziegielewski, Garbharran, and Langowski [1993].

Figure 2.1--Statewide Precipitation and Runoff Deficits

The changes in deliveries from the state's major sources of water provide another perspective on the impact of the drought. Figure 2.3 shows the percentage contribution of the state's sources of supply in 1990, normalized to nondrought conditions.[3] These sources were affected to different degrees by the drought. For example, Colorado River flows into California were maintained at previous levels, although storage on the Lower Colorado River fell over the period. The State Water Project (SWP) and the Central Valley Project (CVP) maintained deliveries from 1987 through 1989 but were forced to implement cutbacks beginning in 1990 when reservoir storage fell to 50 percent of normal levels. SWP and CVP deliveries as a percentage of requests for 1990-1992 are shown in Table 2.1. Ground water pumping increased during the drought, but

---

[3]Retail water agencies obtain water from a variety of sources including agency-owned surface water and ground water; recycled or reclaimed water; local, state, and federal water projects; and wholesale water agencies. In California, most retail water agencies are city-owned or special districts with elected boards, rather than investor-owned, regulated companies. They serve populations that range from less than 100 to over 3,000,000.

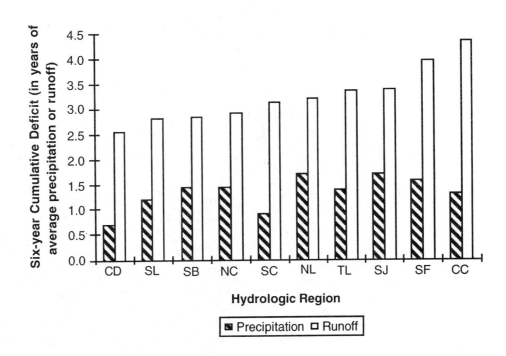

SOURCE: California Department of Water Resources [1991] and Dziegielewski et al. [1993].

NOTE: California's hydrologic regions are abbreviated as follows: Colorado Desert (CD), South Lahontan (Mojave Desert and eastern slope of the Sierras to Mono Lake) (SL), Sacramento (SB), North Coast (NC), South Coast (SC), North Lahontan (eastern slope of the Sierras north of Mono Lake) (NL), Tulare Lake (TL), San Joaquin (SJ), San Francisco Bay (SF), and Central Coast (CC).

Figure 2.2--Precipitation and Runoff Deficits by Hydrologic Region

inadequate recharge caused ground water storage to fall. For example, ground water storage in the San Joaquin Valley is estimated to have fallen by 13 million acre-feet from 1988 through 1992.[4]

---

[4]See California Department of Water Resources [1994], p. 100. There are disadvantages to excessive reliance on ground water basins during droughts. As water levels decline, the amount of energy required to lift the water to the surface increases, water quality may be reduced, land surfaces may subside, and sea water intrusion can be a problem in coastal areas.

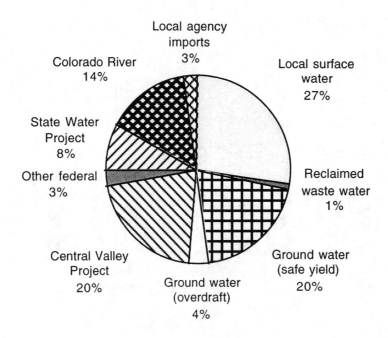

SOURCE: California Department of Water Resources [1994].

Figure 2.3--Sources of Water Supply in 1990

Table 2.1

SWP and CVP Deliveries as a Percentage of Requests

| | State Water Project | | Central Valley Project | |
Year	Agriculture	Urban	Agriculture	Urban
1990	50	100	50	75
1991	0	30	25	50
1992	45	45	25	75

SOURCE: Nash [1993].

The 1991 Drought Water Bank provided an alternative source of supply for local water agencies with critical needs. The California Department of Water Resources purchased water from three sources: temporary surplus in reservoirs (17 percent), surface water supplies freed up by the use of ground water in agricultural areas (33 percent), and surface water supplies freed up by fallowing agricultural lands or dry farming (50 percent). A total of 820,805 acre-feet was purchased at a price of $125 per acre-foot. Water was sold at $175 per acre-foot at the SWP Delta Pumping Plant, with additional charges for conveying water to the place of use. Allocations from the water bank totaled 389,770 acre-feet in 1991, and the remaining water was put into storage.[5] The 1992 Drought Water Bank operated at a smaller scale, mainly using unsold water from the 1991 water bank.[6]

IDENTIFYING AND VALUING DROUGHT EFFECTS

During the 1987-1992 drought, urban water agencies were frequently unable to meet the demands of their customers at prevailing water prices. They were thus forced to develop policies for resolving the imbalance between supply and demand. These policies included a mix of price increases, quantity and type-of-use restrictions, conservation programs, and attempts to augment supplies. The mix of policies chosen determined which users were most affected by water supply shortages and the degree to which they were affected.

Figure 2.4 illustrates how water agency policy translates water supply shortages into changes in actual water use and consumer welfare.[7] The size of the water supply cutbacks, the drought management strategies adopted by water agencies, and customer response to these policies together determine the effect of water supply shortages on consumer welfare.

To identify the effects of the drought management policies adopted by water agencies, one would in principle like to compare what actually happened during the drought with what would have happened had there been

_____

[5]Water bank allocations were less than purchases for several reasons. Some purchased water was used to meet water quality requirements as it moved through the Sacramento-San Joaquin Delta, which interfaces with the San Francisco Bay and salty ocean water. In addition, some of the critical needs that had been anticipated at the time the water was purchased were relieved by unexpectedly heavy rain in March 1991. Unsold water was stored behind Oroville Dam and used in 1992.

[6]See Howitt, Moore, and Smith [1992] and Dixon, Moore, and Schechter [1993] for more information on the Drought Water Bank. Dixon, Moore, and Schechter also provide an analysis of the impact of water sales on the agricultural regions that sold water to the water bank.

[7]Welfare is a term generally used synonymously with happiness or satisfaction in the economics literature. Welfare is determined by the goods and services an individual buys in the market as well nonmarket or nonpriced goods such as clean air, clean water, and public parks. See Just, Hueth, and Schmitz [1982], p. 3.

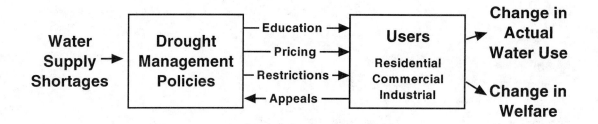

Figure 2.4--Translation of Water Supply Shortages into Reductions in Consumer Welfare

no drought. We can observe what actually happened, but we cannot observe what would have happened had there been no drought, and assuming that all changes observed were due to the drought is probably incorrect. For example, the California economy went into recession toward the end of 1990, and industrial firms were facing increasingly strict enforcement of wastewater treatment standards and potential future liabilities for water pollution.[8] To isolate the effect of the drought on urban users, we need to control for factors other than the drought that affected consumer welfare between 1987 and 1992.

To determine the overall welfare losses in urban areas due to the drought, the identified effects of drought management policies must then be valued. One measure of changes in welfare that is widely used in the economics literature is willingness-to-pay.[9] In the context of the drought, this measure of loss is defined as the maximum dollar amount individuals would have been willing to pay to avoid the drought management strategies adopted by water agencies.[10] Because the utility of money varies across individuals, two individuals may experience the same dollar value of losses (as measured by willingness-to-pay), but their actual changes in welfare may be very different. Thus, summing willingness-to-pay across individuals does not measure the change in overall well-being. However, adding up willingness-to-pay across

---

[8]Adopting new wastewater treatment technologies usually makes disposal of wastewater more expensive and thus may reduce industrial demand for intake water.

[9]See for example Just, Hueth, and Schmitz [1982].

[10]In economics terminology, the maximum amount a consumer or firm would have been willing to pay is called the compensating variation.

individuals does give a measure of how much society would be willing to invest to avoid similar drought management policies in the future and thus is a useful analytic concept.

Below, we first discuss how various drought management policies generate a willingness-to-pay among residential users. We then discuss the effects of drought management policies on business firms and how these effects translate into willingness-to-pay first by individuals who receive firm profits and then by individuals who receive wages and salaries from the firm. Finally, we briefly discuss approaches to quantifying willingness-to-pay.

The Effect of Drought Management Policies for Residential Use on Willingness-to-Pay

As mentioned above, water agencies adopted a wide variety of strategies to reduce water use during the drought, including type-of-use restrictions, price increases, quantity restrictions, and conservation programs. We now discuss how the most common of these policies translate into willingness-to-pay by residential users to avoid the drought management programs adopted by urban water agencies.

Type-of-Use Restrictions. Many water agencies adopt type-of-use restrictions during periods of drought. Examples include prohibitions on washing off driveways and sidewalks, irrigating residential lots during the day, and allowing water from sprinklers to flow into gutters. Although some consumers are unaffected by these restrictions, those whose behavior is constrained are worse off under type-of-use restrictions. If they observe the restrictions, they forgo the net benefits of some water uses. If they do not observe the restrictions, they risk being caught and paying penalties.[11] Consumers consequently would be willing to pay some amount to avoid these restrictions.

_____

[11] During the 1986-1992 drought, the penalty for violating a type-of-use restriction was usually a fine. These fines typically increased with each successive violation, culminating, at least in principle, in the installation of flow restrictors or the termination of water service. In deciding whether to observe a type-of-use restriction or not, a consumer must trade off the probability of being caught multiplied by the fine with the net benefit (benefit minus water cost) of engaging in the restricted activity.

The magnitude of the willingness-to-pay to avoid type-of-use restrictions is presumably a function of the type of restrictions, how often the user engaged in the restricted activity prior to the drought, the probability of being caught, and the penalty if caught.

Price Increases. Water agencies may attempt to reduce residential water consumption by increasing water prices, or they may raise prices to cover higher unit costs resulting from reduced water deliveries. The loss to the consumer due to a price increase consists of two parts. First, the consumer pays more for a given amount of water than he or she would have before the price increase. Second, the higher price will presumably cause the consumer to use less water, and the consumer forgoes the net benefit of water that is no longer consumed. To avoid these losses, consumers would be willing to pay the sum of the increased water costs on units consumed during the drought plus the forgone net benefit of the reduced water use.[12]

Quantity Restrictions. Water agencies may restrict the amount of water that a household can buy in a given period. If this restriction is binding and observed by the household, there is clearly a loss to the household. The household loses the net benefits of the forgone water use and would be willing to pay a positive amount to avoid the restriction.

To enforce quantity restrictions, agencies often adopt surcharges on household water use above the allowed maximum. These surcharges in effect create an increasing block-rate price schedule and make the quantity restriction resemble a type of price increase. These types of quantity restrictions thus generate willingness-to-pay as described previously for price changes. Some agencies also adopt increasingly severe fines for violating quantity restrictions culminating in the installation of flow restrictors or service cutoff. The cost of such penalties increases the consumer's willingness-to-pay to avoid the restrictions.

When deciding whether to observe quantity restrictions, consumers presumably weigh the forgone benefits of reduced consumption with the

---

[12] Both types of welfare losses to residential consumers are described more fully in the discussion of consumer surplus below.

penalties and surcharges. Giving consumers the choice of violating quantity restrictions, even with substantial penalties or surcharges, will result in a willingness-to-pay to avoid the drought that is no higher and most likely lower than if consumers had no choice but to obey quantity restrictions. Consumers may be better off in a system with surcharges for overuse because they can choose to consume additional water if they value its use more than the surcharge.

Conservation Programs. Water agencies often adopt a variety of water conservation programs during times of short supply. When analyzing willingness-to-pay it is useful to divide these programs into two types: device distribution programs and education programs.

Device distribution programs usually involve free distribution of low-flow shower heads, toilet dams, or toilet leak detectors and sometimes sizable rebates for installing ultra-low-flush (ULF) toilets. In deciding whether to install the conservation devices or not, the consumer presumably weighs device and installation costs and any expected reduction in satisfaction from water use (for example, decreased water flow from a low-flow shower head) with the behavioral changes that would be made if the devices were not installed (for example, shorter showers).[13] Consumers presumably also consider water costs and the probability of violating drought quantity restrictions with and without the conservation devices and weigh the benefits and costs over time--both for the expected duration of the drought and subsequent periods when drought management strategies are not in effect.[14] Device distribution programs are voluntary and presumably reduce the negative effects of the drought management programs as measured by willingness-to-pay.

Education programs can take many different forms. Common are public education programs such as bill inserts; television, radio, and newspaper announcements; school programs; and public displays. Agencies

---

[13] Expected reductions in satisfaction due to conservation devices may not actually materialize, however.

[14] Devices that are easily removed, for example low-flow showerheads, may also be replaced by the consumer when drought management policies are suspended.

may also provide individual water audits to identify water saving possibilities at little or no cost.

Public education programs may reduce consumers' willingness-to-pay to avoid drought management strategies in several ways. First, they may decrease willingness-to-pay by providing information that would otherwise be difficult for consumers to obtain and may enable consumers to better control their water use. For example, by learning the major water uses in their home, consumers may be better able to identify low-value water uses that they can cut back with little negative effect. Second, public education programs may reduce willingness-to-pay by increasing consumer awareness of the environmental consequences of diverting water to urban areas during a drought (e.g., if they were told the additional water would come from environmentally sensitive areas).[15] Third, public education programs may reduce willingness-to-pay by making water saving practices the norm. Because everyone is restricting particular uses, for example, an individual's willingness-to-pay to avoid type-of-use restrictions may be reduced. Conversely, there may be an additional "moral cost" of continuing restricted water uses when neighbors are cutting back.

Willingness-to-Pay Induced by Drought Management Strategies for Business

Willingness-to-pay can also be used to measure the effect of drought management policies on business firms. These policies primarily affect firms that use water as a production input, or as part of the goods or services they provide. Water supply cutbacks may affect the incomes of individuals who work for these firms, individuals who receive firm profits, and consumers who buy the firms' products.

We first turn our attention to individuals who receive firm profits. As discussed in subsequent sections, many of the drought management policies applied to residential consumers were also applied to businesses. These policies may affect firm profitability, although to widely varying degrees. For example, restrictions on washing down hard surfaces may have little effect on firm profitability, but water

---

[15] In economics terminology, the ecosystem health would be an argument in individual utility functions.

price increases may have a more significant effect. Profits may fall in the face of higher prices both because firms must pay a higher cost for a given amount of water, and also because higher water costs may cause the firms to reduce the amount of water consumed and production levels, eliminating the profit from units that are no longer produced.

Drought management policies may also reduce the incomes of individuals who earn wages and salaries at firms if they cause firms to cut back on work hours or lay off workers. For workers whose hours are cut back, the willingness-to-pay is a function of the reduction in earnings. For workers who are laid off, the cost of finding a new job (including moving costs), the lost income during the period of unemployment, and any difference between the wages of the new and old jobs also contribute to the willingness-to-pay.

Firms may not only be directly affected by drought management strategies, but indirectly affected. Drought management strategies may reduce the demand for a firm's product and consequently its profits and wages and salaries. For example, restrictions on outdoor watering by residential users may decrease the demand for landscape services and reduce profits, wages, and salaries in the landscaping industry.

Consumers may be adversely affected by increases in product prices due to the drought. Some firms may be able to pass on higher water costs to the consumer or a reduction in production may force product prices up. Consumers would be willing to pay to avoid these price increases.

Finally, it is important to note that some firms will be favorably affected by the drought and others may find some adverse impacts reversed once the drought has ended. For example, demand for certain goods, such as water conservation devices, will likely increase, and the companies that produce them will benefit from increased sales. And, after the drought is over, there may be unusually high demand for nursery products and landscaping services.

Quantifying Willingness-to-Pay

There are two basic approaches to quantifying the willingness-to-pay to avoid the consequences of water supply shortages. First, individuals can be surveyed to directly elicit willingness-to-pay. Individuals can be asked how much they would have paid to avoid the negative effects of the 1986-1992 drought or of a hypothetical drought of similar characteristics.[16] Second, estimates of water demand relationships--the relationship between water price, household income, drought management strategies, other variables, and household water use--and labor supply relationships can be used as the basis for analytically determining willingness-to-pay. (See Moore, Pint, and Dixon [1993], pp. 27-32.)

Both approaches have advantages and drawbacks. The advantage of the survey approach is that it directly focuses on the question of interest and can measure willingness-to-pay caused by all different types of impacts, whether reductions in hours worked caused by business slowdown or drought management policies targeted at the home. One disadvantage is that respondents do not actually have to make the payments they report and thus may over- or understate their willingness-to-pay to avoid the drought. A second disadvantage is that respondents may have little experience valuing these types of losses and may not give realistic answers.

Demand curve analysis offers the promise of measuring willingness-to-pay more quickly and more cheaply than the survey approach, but it has several drawbacks and limitations. First, the demand curve approach will be inexpensive if preexisting demand relations can be used in the analysis. However, these relationships may not accurately capture consumption responses to the various policies adopted during the drought because the range of variation in prices and other policies is much larger during a drought. Thus, time-consuming empirical work using data on water use during the drought may be necessary. In the following paragraphs, we describe how demand curve analysis can be used to estimate the willingness-to-pay to avoid drought management policies.

---

[16] See for example Carson and Mitchell [1987] or Barakat & Chamberlin, Inc. [1994].

Using Demand Analysis to Estimate Willingness-to-Pay

The willingness-to-pay to avoid certain drought management policies can by measured by the change in consumer surplus due to the policy.[17] Consumer surplus is a measure of the difference between the total value households place on the water they consume and the amount they must pay for it. When a drought causes quantity restrictions or price increases, for example, changes in consumer surplus can be used to approximate willingness-to-pay to avoid those policies.

Figure 2.5 illustrates how demand curves can be used to calculate the change in consumer surplus due to a quantity restriction in the absence of changes in other drought management strategies. For each price (p), the demand curve shows the quantity of water (q) that the household wants to buy. The demand curve is downward-sloping because the higher the price of water, the less the household wants to buy. It also shows the relationship between the quantity of water and the household's willingness to pay for an additional unit. The more water the household uses, the less it is willing to pay for an additional unit. The difference between the willingness-to-pay and the actual price is the consumer surplus, or net benefit to the household. Therefore, when the household is free to buy as much water as it wants, the area under the demand curve and above the dashed line at the price p_0 (including both the white and shaded areas) in Figure 2.5 equals the total consumer surplus for the residential household at price p_0.

In Figure 2.5, the household wants to buy a quantity q_0 of water when the price is p_0. Suppose that during the drought, the water agency imposed a quantity restriction that kept the price at p_0 but allowed the household to buy only a quantity of q_1. The difference between the willingness to pay (as represented by the demand curve) and the price is the loss of consumer surplus on each unit of water between q_0 and q_1. Therefore, the area of the triangle ABC represents the household's welfare loss from the drought, as measured by its willingness-to-pay to

---

[17] Consumer surplus only approximates willingness-to-pay, and it becomes a better approximation the smaller the income effect, i.e., the effect of a change of income on water use. (See Just, Hueth, and Schmitz [1982], p. 114.) We equate consumer surplus and willingness-to-pay in the following analysis.

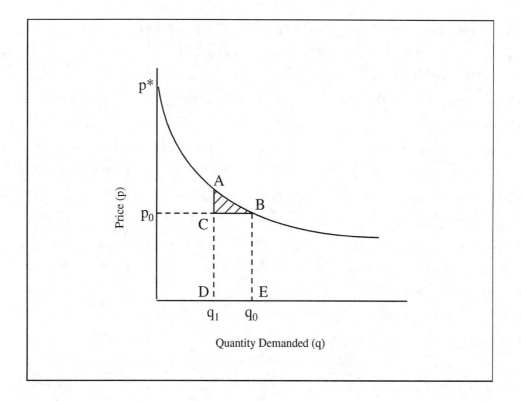

Figure 2.5--Consumer Surplus Loss Due to Quantity Restriction

get the same amount of water it would have purchased in the absence of the drought, minus the previous cost of the water. The diagram also shows the resulting reduction in revenue to the water agency. Before the drought, the quantity charge would have been p_0 x q_0, but now the household pays only p_0 x q_1. Thus, the loss in revenue is represented by the area BCDE.

Similarly, the effect of a price increase during the drought (in the absence of changes in other drought management policies) is shown in Figure 2.6. If the price goes up from p_0 to p_1, the household reduces the amount of water it purchases from q_0 to q_1. The loss of consumer surplus from the reduction in water use, or the "deadweight loss," is given by the area of the triangle BCD. However, the household is also paying a higher price for all of the water it continues to purchase, so it also loses the area of the rectangle ABDE. This part of the loss represents a transfer from the household to the water agency, because it is collected as revenue. The sum of these two areas, ABCDE, represents the total consumer surplus losses and thus is an estimate of the willingness-to-pay to avoid a price increase.

The water agency loses revenue CDFG because of reduced water purchases by the household, but it gains revenue ABDE on the remaining units bought by the household. Thus, the net effect on water agency finances is ABDE – CDFG, which could be positive or negative, depending on the sensitivity of demand to the price charged. In any case, water agency revenues would be higher than if the agency imposed the equivalent quantity restriction. Note that most water agencies had to raise water rates either during or after the drought to make up for losses incurred due to reductions in revenue. These rate increases are a component of drought-related customer losses; however, they are transferred to water agencies, so they are not a loss for society as a whole.

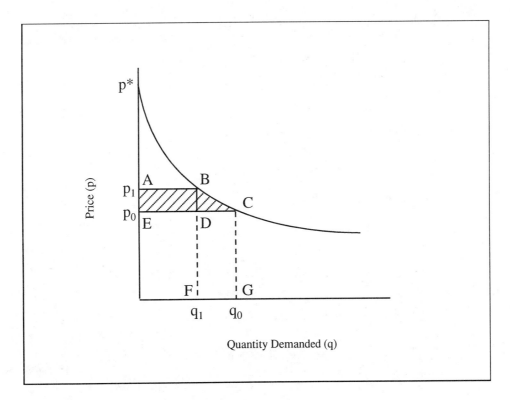

Figure 2.6--Consumer Surplus Loss Due to Price Increase

Measuring changes in areas under an estimated demand curve does not work well to measure the willingness-to-pay to avoid all types of drought management policies. For example, type-of-use restrictions could conceivably curtail some very high-value uses (i.e., uses with values to the left of point B in Figure 2.6). However, demand curve analysis assumes that the lowest value uses are cut back first (i.e., values between points B and C). Standard consumer surplus calculations may thus tend to understate the willingness-to-pay to avoid type-of-use restrictions.[18]

As discussed above, some drought management programs, such as public education or device distribution, may reduce consumers' willingness-to-pay to avoid drought management strategies. These policies may shift the entire demand curve to the left, as shown in Figure 2.7. The change in consumer surplus due to drought management strategies should then be calculated using the new demand curves. In Figure 2.7, the shift in demand results in a smaller consumer surplus loss (area ABC) for the same quantity restriction that was shown in Figure 2.5. As will be illustrated by the analysis in Section 5, it can be very difficult to identify shifts in demand curves; however, if the demand curve has shifted, using the original demand curve could lead to overestimates of the willingness-to-pay.

Drought Effects over Time

In concluding this discussion of a conceptual framework for evaluating drought effects, we briefly discuss valuing drought effects over time. Even though consumers can adjust consumption patterns very quickly, they likely can implement conservation techniques that minimize the losses from reduced consumption only gradually over time. Thus, it

---

[18] Some contingent valuation studies indicate a substantial shortage-related threshold effect (analogous to a large fixed cost to customers of being put into a water shortage situation) that is not related to the magnitude of water cutbacks. This type of effect could not be measured with demand curve analysis.

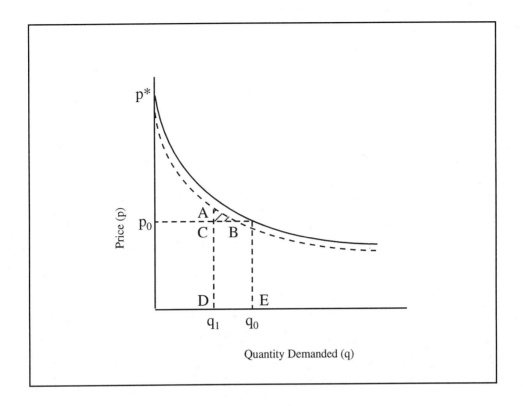

Figure 2.7--Impact of a Demand Shift on Consumer Surplus Loss

is reasonable to expect that the negative effects of drought management policies would be greatest at first and then decline somewhat over time as individuals adapt. This suggests that, ideally, measures of drought effects should look for responses over time that reduce consumer willingness-to-pay (e.g., installing water-efficient appliances or drought-tolerant landscaping) to avoid the consequences of water supply shortages.

3. CHANGE IN WATER USE DURING THE DROUGHT

This section presents findings on water use in a sample of urban water agencies across California between 1986 and 1991. As discussed in Section 2, these changes are the result of the full range of factors affecting water use. In addition to the drought management strategies adopted by water agencies, these factors include changes in weather, the overall economy, population, and industrial wastewater discharge regulations. To the extent possible, we make inferences in this section on the importance of the various factors in explaining changes in water use.

The basis for the analysis is a survey conducted in 1993 of 85 California urban water agencies. We first discuss the survey and the characteristics of the responding agencies. We then examine trends in aggregate water use and water use by customer class. The customer classes examined are residential, commercial, industrial, public authority/institutional, and agricultural/horticultural. Residential use is in turn broken down into single-dwelling unit and multiple-dwelling unit use.

DATA COLLECTION

In 1993, we fielded a survey on water use and drought management policies for the years between 1986 and 1991, and received responses from 85 urban water agencies scattered across California. We collected data for this period because 1986 was the last normal water year before the 1987-1992 drought began and 1991 was the last full year for which data were available at the time of the survey.

Below, we describe our survey approach, sample selection, response rates, and the characteristics of the sample.

Survey Approach

We conducted a mail survey with telephone follow-up of a sample of urban water agencies in California. The questionnaire[1] asked for detailed information on

- water agency revenues
- number of customer accounts by customer class (residential, commercial, industrial, etc.)
- water supplies and deliveries by customer class
- drought management programs
- water rates
- deliveries and use of water from the 1991 Drought Water Bank.

Annual data were collected for all variables except water deliveries. Quarterly data were collected for water deliveries for two reasons. First, agencies report water use over water years that end in different months, and we wanted to obtain a consistent time-profile of water use across agencies. Second, water use is highly seasonal, and quarterly data might allow us to identify different responses to the drought in summer and in winter.

To test the survey instrument, we sent the survey to 10 agencies in the fall of 1992 and received six responses. The instrument was revised based on these responses, but only minor changes were necessary.

Sample Selection

The survey sample was drawn from a list provided by the California Department of Water Resources (DWR) of 684 water agencies in California that distribute drinking water to the public. This list includes all agencies that serve populations over 3,000 and provide over 3,000 acre-feet per year, as well as some smaller agencies. Because we did not want to spend limited survey resources on agencies with relatively few customers, we decided to drop from the list agencies serving populations less than 10,000. DWR, however, did not have population data for all the agencies, so we added agency population provided by the Office of Drinking Water in California's Department of Health Services to the DWR

---

[1]The survey instrument is attached as Appendix A.

list.[2] We were able to determine the population served by 493 of the 684 agencies. Of these, we retained the 338 that served populations of 10,000 or more and dropped the 155 that served populations less than 10,000. From an examination of agency names, it appeared that the 191 agencies for which population data were not available were predominantly small, so they were dropped from consideration.

We drew a sample of 200 using a proportionate sampling technique, in which the probability of being selected was proportional to the population served by the agency. Table 3.1 shows that 87 of the 207 agencies serving populations between 10,000 and 50,000 were selected (42 percent), as were 58 of the 75 agencies serving populations between 50,001 and 100,000 (77 percent), and 55 of the 56 agencies serving populations greater than 100,000 (98 percent).

Table 3.1
Number of Agencies Surveyed and Response Rate

		Pretest		Survey		
	All Water Agencies[a]	Sampled	Respon-dents	Sampled	Respon-dents	Percent-age Respond-ing
Total	338	10	6	200	79	40
Agency Population (thousands)						
10 to 50	207	5	3	87	22	25
51 to 100	75	5	3	58	27	47
> 100	56	0	0	55	30	54
Region						
Bay Area[b]	51	3	1	30	16	53
So. Calif.[c]	182	7	5	117	44	38
Rest of state	105	0	0	53	19	36

[a]Agencies with service area populations greater than 10,000.

[b]Alameda, Contra Costa, San Mateo, San Francisco, Marin, Santa Clara, and Sonoma Counties.

[c]Los Angeles, Orange, Riverside, San Bernardino, San Diego, and Ventura Counties.

---

[2]The Office of Drinking Water in California's Department of Health Services lists 1,250 water agencies that distribute drinking water and have over 200 service connections.

Survey Implementation and Response Rate

We mailed the survey in February 1993. To encourage agencies to commit the considerable resources necessary to complete the survey, an initial contact letter describing the project was sent by the general managers of the CUWA member agencies. RAND staff then contacted the sampled agencies by telephone asking the initial contact person to designate a staff member to receive the survey and be responsible for returning it. RAND staff made follow-up telephone calls to nonrespondents over a period of several months. Rather than fill out the entire survey themselves, most agencies enclosed materials that contained parts of the information requested. We then abstracted the information onto the survey forms.

When the survey period was closed in July 1993, 79 of the 200 sampled agencies had responded (40 percent). This relatively low response rate was due in part to the length of the survey and in part to the type of information requested. Many agencies did not keep records of some of the information requested, and in many cases considerable effort was required to construct it. As will become apparent in the following sections, many agencies only partially completed the survey. Our experience illustrates the difficulty of assembling the data needed to evaluate the effects of the drought.

The response rate varied by agency location and population. As shown in Table 3.1, the response rate was higher in the Bay Area than other parts of the state and higher in agencies with larger service area populations. Large agencies in the sample were not disproportionately located in the Bay Area so both location and population appear to be important in explaining response rates.

Characteristics of Responding Agencies

Because the survey instrument used in the pretest was very similar to the final survey instrument, we added the six agencies responding to the pretest to the 79 agencies responding to the survey for the purposes of analysis. Table 3.2 reports the breakdown of the resulting 85 responding agencies by location and population. The responding agencies are distributed fairly evenly by population. This contrasts with the

Table 3.2

**Distribution of 85 Responding Agencies by
Location and Size (Percent)**

Location	Agency Population (1000s)			All Sizes
	10 to 50	51 to 100	> 100	
Bay Area	2	8	9	20
So. Calif.	22	15	20	58
Rest of state	5	12	6	22
All locations	29	35	35	100

distribution of all urban water agencies with populations of at least 10,000, which, as shown in Table 3.1, is heavily weighted toward agencies serving smaller populations. The difference is due to the oversampling of larger agencies. Most of the responding agencies (58 percent) are in Southern California, but this corresponds fairly closely with the distribution of all urban water agencies with populations of at least 10,000 (see Table 3.1).

Even though the number of water agencies responding to the survey is not large relative to the total number of water agencies in the state, the responding agencies account for a sizable proportion of the total state population. Only 60 of the 85 responding agencies were able to estimate the population in their retail area, but the population served by these 60 agencies was 36 percent of the total state population. (See Table 3.3.) A higher percentage of the Bay Area population was covered by the responding agencies, and, as expected, the vast majority of the population in the responding agencies was in those agencies with the largest populations.

A sizable proportion of total urban water use is provided by the responding agencies. As shown in Table 3.4, the 65 agencies that were able to provide information on water use supplied 26 percent of urban water use in the state. The coverage ranged from 37 percent in the Bay Area to 10 percent in the rest of the state, and, again, the vast bulk of the water was supplied by agencies with the largest populations.

Table 3.3

**1991 Population for Respondents Reporting Population
and All Water Agencies
(N=60)**

| | Number Reporting Population | Population (1000s) | | |
		Respondents	All Water Agencies[a]	Percent-age
Total	60	11,113	30,646	36
Region				
Bay Area	13	3,332	5,665	59
So. California	31	6,121	17,511	35
Rest of state	16	1,660	7,470	22
Agency population (thousands)				
< 10	0	0	NA	NA
10 to 50	15	517	NA	NA
51 to 100	22	1,651	NA	NA
> 100	23	8,945	NA	NA

NA = Not Available.
[a]California Department of Finance [1992], p. 13.

In the remainder of this section, we describe changes in water use by region and by customer class, based on survey responses.

AGGREGATE URBAN WATER USE

As shown in Panel A of Table 3.5, overall water use for the 53 agencies that were able to provide data on water use and population was fairly stable between 1986 and 1990 but then dropped significantly in 1991.[3] Population grew steadily during this period, with the result

---

[3]Throughout this report, we sum various measures of water use and conservation program activity across the agencies in the sample. Thus, larger agencies have more influence on changes over time than smaller agencies. In evaluating overall urban water use in California, this seems appropriate because larger agencies account for a greater proportion of water use than smaller agencies. We have not reweighted our sample to adjust for differences in sampling and response rates by agency population or region. Further work is necessary to determine if such reweighting would change our results significantly.

Table 3.4

1991 Water Use for Respondents Reporting Water Use
for Urban Agencies and All Water Agencies
(N=65)

	Number Reporting Water Use	Water Use (1000s of acre-feet)[a]		Percent-age
		Respondents	All Water Agencies[b]	
Total	65	1,995	7,800	26
Region				
Bay Area	14	480	1,300[c]	37
So. California	37	1,266	4,000[d]	32
Rest of state	14	249	2,500	10
Agency population (thousands)				
< 10	0	0	NA	NA
10 to 50	16	92	NA	NA
51 to 100	23	255	NA	NA
> 100	26	1,648	NA	NA

NA = Not Available.
[a]One acre-foot is approximately 326,000 gallons.
[b]California Department of Water Resources (1994), p. 156.
[c]San Francisco Hydrologic Region.
[d]South Coast Hydrologic Region.

that per-capita water use fell 5 percent between 1986 and 1990, and another 14 percent in 1991. (See the last column of Table 3.5, Panel A.)

There was some variation in changes in water use across the state. Per-capita water use in Southern California changed little between 1986 and 1990 but then dropped 16 percent in 1991. (See Panel B of Table 3.5.) A similar pattern occurred in the rest of the state (areas outside Southern California and the Bay Area) although the declines between 1986 and 1990 were somewhat larger and the drop in 1991 was not as severe. (See Panel D of Table 3.5.) Per-capita water use dropped earlier in the Bay Area: As shown in Panel C of Table 3.5, water use fell significantly in 1988 and 1989, and then dropped another 12 percent in 1991.

Table 3.5
Water Use in Responding Urban Water Agencies
in California and Its Regions
(N=53)

	Total Water Use (1000s of acre-feet)	Percent- age Change	Population (1000s)	Percent- age Change	Water Use per capita (acre-feet per capita)	Percent- age Change
A. California (N=53)						
1986	1,806	---	9,659	---	0.187	---
1987	1,855	2.7	9,852	2.0	0.188	0.7
1988	1,828	-1.5	10,044	1.9	0.182	-3.2
1989	1,840	0.7	10,206	1.6	0.180	-1.1
1990	1,840	0	10,376	1.7	0.177	-1.7
1991	1,611	-12.4	10,550	1.7	0.153	-13.6
B. Southern California (N=28)						
1986	1,049	---	5,328	---	0.197	---
1987	1,070	2.0	5,464	2.6	0.196	-0.6
1988	1,092	2.1	5,552	1.6	0.197	0.5
1989	1,136	4.0	5,671	2.1	0.200	1.5
1990	1,127	-0.8	5,768	1.7	0.195	-2.5
1991	966	-14.3	5,890	2.1	0.164	-15.9
C. Bay Area (N=12)						
1986	504	---	3,037	---	0.166	---
1987	528	4.8	3,061	0.8	0.173	3.9
1988	470	-10.0	3,079	0.6	0.153	-11.6
1989	436	-7.2	3,092	0.4	0.141	-7.8
1990	450	3.2	3,116	0.8	0.144	2.1
1991	398	-11.5	3,132	0.5	0.127	-11.8
D. Rest of state (N=13)						
1986	253	---	1,294	---	0.195	---
1987	257	1.5	1,326	2.5	0.194	-0.9
1988	266	3.5	1,412	6.5	0.189	-2.6
1989	268	0.8	1,442	2.1	0.186	-1.6
1990	264	-1.5	1,493	3.5	0.177	-4.8
1991	247	-6.4	1,527	2.3	0.162	-8.5

Per-capita water use in Southern California and in the rest of the state were similar at the beginning and end of this period--starting at approximately 0.20 acre-feet per capita in 1986 and dropping to approximately 0.16 acre-feet per capita in 1991. Per-capita water use in the Bay Area was substantially lower, however. Its 1986 value was close to the 1991 level in the other parts of the state and fell to 0.13 acre-feet in 1991. These differences presumably reflect differences between the Bay Area and other parts of the state in types of housing, weather, and conservation efforts.

Even though these changes in aggregate per-capita water use reflect the changes in the full panoply of factors affecting water use, in Section 4 we will see that these declines correspond in time to the drought management policies adopted by water agencies. The sudden decline in overall water use in 1991 thus suggests that the drought management programs did have an effect throughout the state in 1991. The pattern of water use in the Bay Area suggests that the drought affected the Bay Area starting in 1988.

The following analysis describes the statewide effect of the drought, so we will focus on the change in water use in 1991.

URBAN WATER USE BY CUSTOMER CLASS

As shown in Table 3.6, residential use accounted for almost two-thirds of total urban water use in 1986, with use by single-dwelling units roughly twice as large as that by multiple-dwelling units. Commercial businesses accounted for 21 percent of use, and the industrial and public authority/institutional sectors accounted for roughly 5 percent. Only 1 percent of water supplied by urban agencies went to agricultural/horticultural users in 1986.[4] This suggests that, when determining aggregate willingness-to-pay to avoid the drought in urban areas, residential use is of primary concern. Next in importance is the commercial sector. The industrial and public authority/ institutional sectors may make some contribution but probably not much, and changes in agricultural/horticultural uses will likely have little effect on the overall willingness-to-pay.

---

[4]These proportions are similar to those reported by Metropolitan Water District of Southern California [1990], p. 27, although the percentage consumed by single-dwelling units in this report is somewhat greater.

Table 3.6

Breakdown of Water Use by Customer Class
(N=44, in percentage)

	1986	1991
Residential	64	64
Single-dwelling unit	41	40
Multiple-dwelling unit	23	24
Commercial	21	21
Industrial	5	5
Public authority/institutional	6	5
Agricultural/horticultural	1	1
Other	3	3
Total	100	100

Surprisingly, there was very little change in the breakdown of water use by customer class between 1986 and 1991. At first thought, this might suggest that the drought similarly affected the various customer classes. However, this comparison does not control for differing growth rates in the various sectors and other confounding factors that differentially affected customer classes, such as changes in industrial wastewater discharge standards. It also may be that the willingness-to-pay to avoid a given cutback varies a great deal across sectors. To develop a better understanding of how the drought effects varied by customer class, we now investigate changes in water use by customer class.

Residential Water Use

Residential water use in the responding agencies remained stable through 1990 but then fell 14 percent in 1991 (see Panel A of Table 3.7). When adjusted for population growth, residential use fell somewhat between 1986 and 1990 but dropped approximately 15 percent in 1991. This closely mirrors the change in total use per capita, as ought to be expected because residential use accounts for almost two-thirds of overall use.

Table 3.7

**Residential Water Deliveries by Type of Dwelling Unit, As Reported
by Urban Water Agencies in California**

	Total Water Use (1000s of acre-feet)	Percent- age Change	Pop- ulation (1000s)	Percent- age Change	Water Use Per Capita (acre-feet per capita)	Percent- age Change
A. All Dwelling Units (N=40)						
1986	1,057	---	8,635	---	0.122	---
1987	1,089	3.0	8,795	1.8	0.123	1.2
1988	1,061	-2.6	8,937	1.6	0.119	-3.3
1989	1,063	0.2	9,033	1.1	0.118	-0.8
1990	1,053	-0.9	9,146	1.3	0.115	-2.5
1991	905	-14.1	9,267	1.3	0.098	-14.8
			Accounts		per Account	
B. Single-Dwelling Units (N=25)						
1986	506	---	1,185	---	0.427	---
1987	518	2.4	1,199	1.2	0.432	1.1
1988	503	-2.9	1,187	-1.0	0.424	-1.9
1989	502	-0.2	1,198	0.9	0.420	-0.9
1990	487	-3.0	1,209	0.9	0.402	-4.3
1991	393	-19.3	1,216	0.6	0.324	-19.4
C. Multiple-Dwelling Units (N=22)						
1986	276	---	148	---	1.86	---
1987	280	1.6	149	0.8	1.88	0.8
1988	280	0.0	151	1.3	1.85	-1.6
1989	286	2.1	153	1.3	1.87	1.1
1990	279	-2.4	155	1.3	1.80	-3.7
1991	245	-12.2	156	0.6	1.56	-13.3

One factor other than the drought that may have contributed to the sharp decline in residential water use in 1991 is the economic recession that hit California at the end of 1990. Table 3.8 shows that per-capita wages and salaries adjusted for inflation fell almost 5 percent in 1991, and because residential water use is affected by household income, this drop in real income could have caused a drop in water use. The drop in income, however, is not nearly enough to explain the drop in residential water use. The income elasticity for water demand is generally thought to be substantially less than one even in the long run, which means that the decline in income would have reduced residential water use by less

Table 3.8

**Percentage Change in California Wages and Salaries
and Population**

	Real Wages and Salaries	Population	Real Wages and Salaries Per Capita
1986	---	---	---
1987	4.9	2.2	2.7
1988	3.7	2.5	1.1
1989	2.1	2.5	-0.4
1990	1.6	3.1	1.4
1991	-2.8	2.0	-4.7

SOURCE: California Department of Finance [1993], pp. 10, 52, and 60. Wages adjusted using consumer price index.

than 5 percent.[5] Other confounding factors need to be examined, such as changes in weather, but it is likely that a substantial portion of the 14 percent drop in per-capita residential consumption was due to the drought management programs adopted by water agencies. This suggests that the drought management programs for residential use generated a willingness-to-pay to avoid the consequences of such programs.

The declines in use per account were larger for single-dwelling units than multiple-dwelling units (see Panels B and C of Table 3.7).[6] The difference is substantial and suggests that drought management programs targeted single-dwelling units or that single-dwelling units were more responsive to the programs.[7] Greater cutbacks by single-

---

[5]For example, Griffin and Chang (1990) report income elasticities for water demand between 0.30 and 0.48, and Sewell and Roueche (1974) report an elasticity of 0.19. Household income may have a greater effect on the household's ability to invest in water-saving appliances and landscaping than on short-term water use. Thus, a recession-related drop in income would not be expected to affect water use substantially in the short run.

[6]The number of people living in multiple- and single-dwelling units was not available, thus multiple- and single-dwelling use is normalized by the number of accounts. The percentage change in the number of accounts over time, however, closely parallels the percentage change in population.

[7]Multiple-dwelling unit users may have been less responsive to drought management programs for several reasons. First, a landlord often pays the water bill for multiple-dwelling units and higher water costs may only appear as rent increases much later. Second, because

dwelling units does not necessarily mean that the willingness-to-pay (adjusted for number of units) is greater for single-dwelling units than multiple-dwelling unit users. Cutbacks by single-dwelling unit users could have been restricted to low-value uses to a greater extent than those by multiple-dwelling unit users. For example, outdoor use accounts for a larger share of total use for single-dwelling units than for multiple-dwelling units, and it may be less painful to reduce outdoor use than indoor use.

Commercial Water Use

Commercial water use fell somewhat between 1986 and 1990 but then fell approximately 11 percent in 1991 (see Panel A of Table 3.9).[8] The decline in commercial water use is likely due in part to agency drought management programs and in part to the recession that hit California at the end of 1990. Even though we found it likely that much of the change in residential water use can be attributed to the drought, there is much more uncertainty about how much of the fall in commercial use is drought-related. The recession may explain a large part of the nearly 3 percent fall in commercial wages and salaries in 1991 (see Table 3.10) as well as some of the decline in commercial water use. At a minimum, the data suggest that declines in commercial water due to the drought are reflected much less than proportionately in wages and salaries, at least for the range of water use reductions observed during the drought.

Another important aspect of drought effects is the effect on firm profits and thus on the individuals who receive profits, such as small business owners and stockholders. Data on profits by sector over this period are not readily available, so we did not investigate the relationship between water cutbacks and changes in profit. It may well be, however, that profits were more affected by changes in water use during the drought than were wages and salaries.[9]

---

there is only one water meter for many users, savings by one user are split among many users. Third, multiple-dwelling unit users may have fewer low-value uses to cut back than single-dwelling unit users.

[8]For completeness, the number of commercial accounts and commercial use per account is also reported in Table 3.9.

[9]If firms expect water supply shortages to be short term, they may want to conserve firm-specific human capital and maintain worker

Table 3.9

Commercial and Industrial Water Deliveries Reported by
Urban Water Agencies in California

	Total Water Use (1000s of acre-feet)	Percent-age Change	Accounts (1000s)	Percent-age Change	Water Use per Account (acre-feet per acct.)	Percent-age Change
A. Commercial (N=37)						
1986	405	---	209	---	1.94	---
1987	414	2.1	215	2.8	1.92	-0.7
1988	401	-3.1	200	-7.0	2.01	4.7
1989	390	-2.7	203	1.5	1.92	-4.5
1990	389	-0.3	206	1.5	1.89	-1.6
1991	346	-11.1	208	1.0	1.67	-11.6
B. Industrial (N=28)						
1986	93.3	---	16.9	---	5.51	---
1987	94.5	1.3	18.1	6.7	5.24	-5.0
1988	94.7	0.2	17.4	-3.9	5.43	3.6
1989	92.1	-2.7	17.6	1.1	5.73	5.5
1990	88.3	-4.1	17.6	0.0	5.03	-12.2
1991	74.5	-15.6	17.4	-1.1	4.27	-15.1

Table 3.10

Percentage Change in Commercial and
Industrial Wages and Salaries in
California
(adjusted for inflation)

	Commercial	Industrial
1986	---	---
1987	6.8	1.8
1988	4.6	2.5
1989	2.4	-0.7
1990	2.7	-2.2
1991	-2.6	-4.1

SOURCE: California Department of
Finance [1993], pp. 52 and 60. Wages
adjusted using consumer price index.

goodwill and thus may be willing to forgo short-term profits before
reducing wages and salaries.

Industrial Water Use

Water agency deliveries to industrial uses fell approximately 5 percent between 1986 and 1990 but then fell more than 15 percent in 1991 (see Panel B of Table 3.9). This decline is as large as the fall in residential use and suggests that industrial users were affected by drought management policies. Some industrial users may have their own groundwater pumps, however, and partially offset reduced water agency deliveries by increased groundwater pumping. The decline in overall industrial use may thus be lower than that reported here. Changes in industrial groundwater use during the drought remain to be examined.

The same problem of disentangling the drought effect from other effects holds for industrial use as for commercial use. As shown in Table 3.10, industrial wages and salaries stagnated between 1986 and 1990 and then dropped 4 percent in 1991. The recession contributed to the decline in industrial water use as did the gradual adoption of industrial wastewater treatment requirements during this period.[10] New treatment requirements make wastewater discharge more expensive and presumably increase incentives to reduce fresh water use. The United States Environmental Protection Agency began issuing treatment technology requirements for the wastewater produced by various industrial processes in 1982.[11] Requirements for different processes were released over time, and California municipalities started to enforce these requirements in 1984 and 1985.[12] The aggressiveness with which these requirements were enforced varied across municipalities: It appears in some cases that there was little enforcement in some agencies until the late 1980s. The lag in enforcement and the release of new requirements over time suggest that these regulations put downward pressure on industrial water use between 1986 and 1991. In particular, this may account for part of the 5 percent decline in industrial water

---

[10] Increased awareness of liability for pollution under the Comprehensive Environmental Response, Compensation, and Liability Act of 1980 (Superfund) may have also been a factor.

[11] The standards were released under the Clean Water Act.

[12] Based on telephone interview with B. Patel, Los Angeles Department of Public Works.

use between 1986 and 1990 that occurred even though industrial wages and salaries rose slightly.

The ratio between the percentage change in industrial water use and industrial wages and salaries between 1990 and 1991 (3.8) is similar to that for commercial users (4.3). This again suggests that, at least for water cutbacks of 15 percent or less, changes in industrial water use are reflected much less than proportionately in the change in wages and salaries, although any increased groundwater pumping remains to be factored in. Industrial profits may also have been affected by the drought, and most likely to a greater degree than wages and salaries.

Public Authority and Institutional Water Use

As shown in Table 3.11, public authority and institutional water use rose slightly between 1986 and 1990 but dropped approximately 23 percent in 1991. The number of public authority and institutional accounts grew rapidly through 1990, and the stability of water use between 1986 and 1990 may have been the result of early adoption of conservation practices.[13] Even though water use dropped sharply in 1991, the number of accounts remained constant.

It seems less likely than for commercial and industrial users that factors other than the drought were major causes of the decline in public authority and in institutional water use. The decline in public authority and institutional water use thus suggests the drought management strategies of public water agencies had a substantial effect on public authority and institutional users. The willingness-to-pay generated by these cutbacks, however, would be difficult to measure. On the one hand, the cutbacks may have been in low-value uses such as water

----

[13] The number of accounts may not be a good measure of the size of the public authority and institutional sectors. According to an expert on such issues, the number of accounts often changes even if the number of buildings physically connected to the water system remains stable. The number of commercial and industrial accounts apparently exhibits less variability. Even when two commercial or industrial firms merge, the separate buildings of the two firms usually remain on separate water meters. (Written communication by Wendy Illingsworth to authors, October 6, 1994.)

Table 3.11

Public Authority/Institutional Water Use Reported by
Water Agencies in California
(N=33)

	Total Water Use (1000s of acre-feet)	Percent-age Change	Accounts (1000s)	Percent-age Change	Water Use per Account (acre-feet per acct.)	Percent-age Change
1986	84.3	---	14.3	---	5.89	---
1987	84.9	0.7	14.9	4.1	5.70	-3.3
1988	85.6	0.8	15.9	6.7	5.37	-5.8
1989	84.2	-1.6	16.3	2.5	5.17	-3.7
1990	87.5	3.9	16.6	1.8	5.27	1.9
1991	67.4	-23.0	16.6	0.0	4.05	-23.1

fountains. On the other hand, the sizable reduction suggests that high-value uses could possibly have been affected.

Agricultural and Horticultural Use

Agricultural and horticultural use experienced the largest relative declines in agency deliveries between 1986 and 1991. (See Table 3.12.) Agricultural and horticultural deliveries were 20 percent lower in 1990 than in 1986 and fell another 25 percent in 1991. This occurred even though the number of agricultural and horticultural accounts remained stable over the period. These declines may have been partially offset by increased groundwater pumping, but further work is needed to determine the extent to which this occurred.

Even though overall agricultural and horticultural water use declined during the drought, factors other than drought management strategies may explain the changes. Urbanization may have reduced the number of acres available to agriculture, even if the number of accounts remained stable. Decreased agricultural crop prices and increased production costs may have also contributed to the decline.[14]

---

[14]Note also that only seven agencies provided data on agricultural/horticultural water use. This is in large part because relatively few agencies made large enough deliveries to this customer class to warrant reporting them separately. Given the small sample size, the significance of the changes reported in Table 3.12 should be interpreted with caution.

Table 3.12

**Agricultural/Horticultural Water Deliveries Reported
by Urban Water Agencies in California
(N=7)**

	Total Water Use (1000s of acre-feet)	Percent-age Change	Accounts (1000s)	Percent-age Change	Water Use per Account (acre-feet per acct.)	Percent-age Change
1986	9.1	---	1.2	---	7.5	---
1987	8.3	-8.9	1.3	10.3	6.2	-17.4
1988	8.3	0.0	1.3	0.0	6.3	1.6
1989	6.7	-19.3	1.3	0.0	5.0	-20.6
1990	7.3	9.0	1.1	-15.4	6.4	28.0
1991	5.5	-24.7	1.3	18.2	4.3	-32.8

The large decline in agricultural and horticultural water deliveries suggests that water supply reductions during the drought may have significantly affected agriculture. Many farmers are on interruptible rates, which provide for a cessation of water deliveries in periods of short supply. Farmers may then have to turn to more expensive groundwater. Losses to nurseries may be even larger than indicated by the drop in water use. Nursery growers may have used water to grow plants but then faced reduced demand for their products during the drought.

SUMMARY

It appears that the bulk of the drought's effects occurred in 1991, although there were likely some negative impacts starting in 1988 in the Bay Area. Table 3.13 summarizes the declines in water use by customer class between 1990 and 1991 and suggests that all customer classes must be examined in assessing the effects of the drought. In terms of the aggregate effect of drought management policies, the impacts on residential and commercial classes are probably most important because between them they account for approximately 85 percent of the water use in our sample. However, policymakers may have special concerns about adverse affects on other sectors that warrant detailed examination.

The decreased use by residential, public authority and institutional users was probably largely due to drought management policies, although we are unable to disentangle the effect of the

Table 3.13

**Percentage Change in Water Use Between 1990 and 1991,
by Customer Class**

Customer Class	Number of Agencies	Percentage Change
Total water use	53	-12.4
Residential	40	-14.1
Single-dwelling unit	25	-19.3
Multiple-dwelling unit	22	-12.2
Commercial	37	-11.1
Industrial	28	-15.6
Public authority/institutional	33	-23.0
Agricultural	7	-24.8

drought from other confounding factors. There is more uncertainty in how much of the commercial, industrial, and agricultural reductions were due to the drought, but it seems likely that the drought was a significant factor.

There is much that could be done to better isolate the drought from other factors. For example, data over a longer period of time on water use, wages and salaries, and the economy could be assembled, or more use could be made of variations in drought management strategies, wages and salaries, and economic conditions across the agencies responding to the survey.

The results suggest that reductions in water use by commercial and industrial users were translated much less than proportionately into changes in wages and salaries. This raises the possibility that commercial and industrial cutbacks did not induce large willingness-to-pay among wage and salary earners. Even though cutbacks in residential use were similar to those by commercial and industrial users, this does not necessarily suggest that residential effects were not large: residential cutbacks may have been far more painful than commercial and industrial cutbacks. More information on *how* the cutbacks were made by the various customer classes would provide a better understanding of the magnitude of willingness-to-pay generated.

In the next section, we investigate the drought management strategies adopted by the responding water agencies. How these strategies varied by customer class will give us a better idea of what sectors were targeted by water agencies and which sectors may have been willing to pay significant amounts to avoid the drought management policies.

4. DROUGHT MANAGEMENT STRATEGIES

In this section we characterize the drought management strategies adopted by the responding agencies between 1986 and 1991. We start by describing agency water use reduction goals during the drought. We examine agency restrictions on the quantity of water used followed by restrictions on particular types of water use. We then turn to water conservation programs and changes in water pricing. Under each topic, we first examine overall agency strategy and then examine the variation in strategy across customer class. We conclude this section by examining supply augmentation strategies, focusing on purchases from the 1991 Drought Water Bank run by the California Department of Water Resources.

WATER USE REDUCTION GOALS

Overall Agency Strategy

A sizable majority of the water agencies responding to the survey set goals for reducing overall customer water use during the drought. Of the 85 respondents, 55 (65 percent) indicated that they set cutback goals at some point during the drought, and some of the others that did not answer this question may have developed goals as well. Among agencies that reported the dates of their water reduction goals (48 of the 55 that set goals), few set goals at the beginning of the period. No agencies reported reduction goals in 1986 and 1987, but the number with reduction goals rose rapidly between 1988 and 1991 (see Table 4.1). Agencies in the Bay Area developed goals earlier than agencies in Southern California or other parts of the state ("rest of the state"). These patterns are consistent with the reductions in water use reported in Section 3 that suggested that negative drought impacts were concentrated in 1991 for Southern California and the rest of the state but occurred earlier in the Bay Area.

The largest agencies in the sample began adopting cutback goals earlier than smaller agencies. This may have been because the largest agencies had more sophisticated planning departments, but it may also

Table 4.1

Number of Agencies Specifying Water Reduction Goals, by Year
(N=48)

	Survey Respondents	Number That Specified Goal					
		1986	1987	1988	1989	1990	1991
All	85	0	0	6	10	25	48
Region							
Bay Area	17	0	0	4	6	10	13
So. California	49	0	0	1	2	13	30
Rest of the state	19	0	0	1	2	2	5
Population (thousands)							
10 to 50	25	0	0	1	2	6	13
51 to 100	30	0	0	1	3	9	16
> 100	30	0	0	4	5	10	19

have been because a greater fraction of the largest agencies that responded to the survey were in the Bay Area. (See Table 3.2 in the previous section.) Further statistical work is needed to isolate the effect of agency size from other factors.[1]

On average, agencies that set water reduction goals in 1991 sought to reduce overall use 15 percent from 1989 levels. (See Table 4.2.) Agencies usually adjusted for growth in the number of accounts, so the desired cutback can be thought of as the desired cutback for each account, on average. The average reduction goal was lower in the Bay Area than either Southern California or the rest of the state, but this may be because drought management strategies had already lowered 1989 use in many Bay Area agencies. Goals were somewhat lower in the largest agencies, but this may be because a greater fraction of the largest agencies that responded are in the Bay Area.

---

[1]Another possibility is that smaller agencies were more easily able to increase groundwater pumping to offset reduced surface water supplies than larger agencies. This conjecture, however, needs to be further examined.

Table 4.2

Water Reduction Goals in 1991
(adjusted to 1989 base year)

	Survey Respondents	Average Requested Cutback[a] (percent)	Minimum Requested Cutback[b] (percent)	Maximum Requested Cutback (percent)
All	42	15.1	-11.9	38.2
Region				
Bay Area	15	10.8	-0.2	21.9
So. Calif.	24	17.8	8.0	23.4
Rest of state	3	15.5	-11.9	38.2
Population (thousands)				
10 to 50	12	16.7	8.0	21.0
51 to 100	13	16.1	-0.2	38.2
> 100	17	13.2	-11.9	23.0

[a]Simple average of responding agencies. In most cases, agencies had in mind a cutback adjusted for growth in number of accounts.

[b]Some entries are negative because the requested cutbacks have been adjusted to a common base year (1989).

Variation by Customer Class

Surprisingly, few agencies appear to have explicitly varied cutback goals by customer class. Cutback goals varied in only 12 of the 55 agencies reporting goals (22 percent). For the 10 agencies that both varied and reported cutback goals by customer class, cutback goals were substantially lower for commercial and industrial users than for residential users (see Table 4.3). Clearly some agencies were attempting to protect their commercial and industrial users from drought management strategies, but our data suggest that only a minority did so explicitly. However, agencies that did not vary requested cutbacks by customer class may have used other policies to protect their commercial and industrial customers. For example, as will be discussed shortly, quantity restrictions may have been less stringent or easier to appeal for commercial and industrial users than for residential users.

Table 4.3

**1991 Water Reduction Goals,
by Customer Class in 1991
(N=10)**

Customer Class	Average Requested Cutback (percent)
Residential	19.9
Commercial	12.5
Industrial	10.8

QUANTITY RESTRICTIONS

Overall Agency Strategy

A sizable proportion of the responding agencies adopted quantity restrictions at some point between 1986 and 1991. Most agencies implemented quantity restrictions in terms of a percentage reduction of use relative to a base year, although some expressed them as an absolute amount over some period of time (gallons per day, for example). Of the 56 agencies answering the survey question on quantity restrictions, 40 (71 percent) reported that they issued quantity restrictions (see Table 4.4). The proportion may have been lower for agencies that did not answer the question, and the last column of Table 4.4 gives a lower bound on the proportion of agencies adopting quantity restrictions for all 85 responding agencies: It assumes that agencies that did not answer the question did not implement quantity restrictions. This lower bound (47 percent) is undoubtedly an underestimate of the actual percentage of agencies adopting quantity restrictions.

Quantity restrictions were mandatory in most cases. Panel A of Table 4.5 shows that 48 percent of the agencies with quantity restrictions adopted mandatory restrictions and that another 34 percent adopted a combination of voluntary and mandatory restrictions. In most cases, the penalty for violating mandatory restrictions was a surcharge on all consumption above the allotment. The surcharge often rose with consumption over the baseline. The surcharge for use in an initial range over the allotment was frequently two or three times the normal unit cost of water, but some agencies set surcharges of up to ten times the normal unit cost for extremely high consumption. Penalties such as

Table 4.4

**Number and Proportion of Agencies Engaged in Various
Drought Management Strategies**

	Engaged in Activity (1)	Did Not Engage in Activity (2)	Did Not Answer Question (3)	Proportion Answering Who Engaged in Activity (1)/ ((1)+(2))	Lower Bound on Proportion Engaged in Activity (1)/Total Responding
Quantity restrictions	40	16	29	71	47
Type-of-use restrictions	55	16	14	77	65
Conservation programs Public education programs	73	3	9	96	86
Water audits	25	44	16	36	29
Conservation kits	65	10	10	87	76
Incentives for ULF toilets	23	50	12	32	27

these result in an increasing block rate structure, where the marginal
cost of an additional unit of water depends on the amount consumed. In
these cases, quantity restrictions look much like changes in rate
structures.

Rate surcharges for exceeding quantity restrictions were sometimes
combined with fines that did not necessarily depend on the excess amount
of water consumed. These fines would increase with the number of
violations, in many cases potentially culminating with the installation
of a flow restrictor or termination of water service. In some cases,
fines alone were used, and there was no surcharge on water use over the
allotment.

Most agencies that adopted quantity restrictions set up a mechanism
that could considerably soften their effects on some customers. Thirty-
six of the 40 agencies (90 percent) reporting quantity restrictions set
up an appeals process whereby customers could request that their
quantity allotments be increased. For example, residential customers
could make an appeal for medical reasons or if the number of residents
had increased since the baseline period. Commercial and industrial

Table 4.5

**Characteristics of Quantity Restrictions
Between 1986 and 1991**

	Percentage of Agencies with Quantity Restriction
A. Enforcement (N=33)	
Mandatory only	48
Voluntary and mandatory	34
Voluntary only	18
B. Customer class targeted (N=40)	
Single-dwelling unit	90
Multiple-dwelling unit	83
Commercial	75
Industrial	67

customers could often make appeals if limiting use to their allotment
would have meant a cutback in employment or output.[2]

Overall, only a small share of customers requested appeals. Four
percent of customers requested exemptions (see last line of Table 4.6),
which were almost always granted (see last line of Table 4.7). As we
will see shortly, a high percentage of customers were assessed penalties
for violating quantity restrictions, so the requested cutbacks were
presumably binding. The low percentage of customers requesting
exemptions thus probably reflects fairly strict requirements to qualify
for an exemption, although some customers may not have considered the
time cost of applying for an exemption worth the expected decrease in
the water bill.

It appears that violations of quantity restrictions were widespread
and that a sizable share of customers were assessed penalties for
violations. Of the 40 agencies that adopted restrictions, 34 (85
percent) assessed penalties for violations. As shown in Panel A of
Table 4.8, the number of penalties assessed was 55 percent of the number
of accounts for the 13 agencies that were able to report both the number
of penalties and the number of accounts. This suggests that roughly
one-half of the customers in districts with mandatory quantity
restrictions violated the quantity restrictions and were assessed

---

[2]See Moore, Pint, and Dixon [1993], p. 10.

penalties.[3] Violators also paid a sizable amount in penalties and surcharges. The average penalty was approximately $40, generating over $24 million just in the 13 agencies providing data (see Panel B of Table 4.8).

Table 4.6

**Exemptions from Quantity Restrictions Requested
Between 1986 and 1991**

	Number of Agencies	Exemptions Requested (1)	Accounts (2)	Percentage of Accounts Requesting Exceptions
Residential	16	22,259	1,497,084	2
Single-dwelling unit	10	13,994	1,062,123	1
Multiple-dwelling unit	10	4,281	187,553	2
Commercial	16	8,748	141,702	6
Industrial	13	1,708	12,774	13
Public authority	12	100	10,833	1
All classes	19	43,466	1,067,323	4

Table 4.7

**Exemptions from Quantity Restrictions Granted
Between 1986 and 1991**

	Number of Agencies	Exemptions Requested (1)	Exemptions Granted (3)	Percentage of Requested Exemptions Granted
Residential	21	23,691	22,285	94
Single-dwelling unit	17	17,604	16,471	94
Multiple-dwelling unit	17	4,488	4,381	98
Commercial	21	8,773	8,006	93
Industrial	22	1,718	1,633	95
Public authority	22	100	100	100
All classes	21	199,105	184,101	93

---

[3]It is likely that there were some repeat violators (each billing period could produce a violation) so the percentage of accounts penalized would have been lower than 55 percent.

Table 4.8

Number of Penalties and Surcharges Assessed for
Quantity Restrictions in 1991
(N=13)

A. Number of Penalties	
Number assessed	614,343
Number of accounts	1,123,952
Ratio of number of penalties assessed to number of accounts	0.55
B. Surcharges assessed	
Amount billed ($1000)	24,384
Number of penalties	603,874
Amount billed per penalty ($)	40.38

These high violation rates suggest real adverse impacts from quantity restrictions and imply that users would have been willing to pay a significant amount to avoid quantity restrictions. The sizable penalties were clearly losses to consumers, although they were transferred to the water agencies and were not lost from a social perspective.[4] The higher per unit water costs created by the penalties would cause users to reduce the amount consumed and thus the net benefits generated. Some users also undoubtedly cut back use, and thus enjoyed fewer benefits of water use, in order to avoid penalties.[5]

Variation by Customer Class

There is evidence that water agencies attempted to shield their commercial and industrial users from severe economic damages during the drought. First, as shown in Panel B of Table 4.5, quantity restrictions were applied less frequently to commercial and industrial users than to residential users. Commercial and industrial users were issued quantity restrictions in 75 percent and 67 percent of agencies issuing quantity restrictions, respectively, compared with 90 and 83 percent for single-dwelling units and multiple-dwelling units. Second, the reduction goals were also lower for commercial and industrial accounts than residential accounts in some agencies (see Table 4.3), although as noted above,

---

[4]They may have been partially used to subsidize conservation programs, a point to which we return below.

[5]The marginal value of water to users who did not incur penalties is presumably lower than that to users who did incur penalties, however.

reduction goals did not vary by customer class for most agencies. Third, a higher percentage of commercial and industrial users requested and were granted exemptions from quantity restrictions than were residential users. (See Tables 4.6 and 4.7.) These three factors resulted in a lower proportion of agencies assessing penalties against commercial and industrial users than against residential users: In agencies that were able to report penalties for violations of quantity restrictions by customer class, 93 percent assessed penalties against residential users compared with 50 percent against commercial users and 36 percent against industrial users. (See Table 4.9.)

Overall the findings suggest that quantity restrictions had widespread negative effects on residential users during the drought but that commercial and industrial users were spared to some extent. Two observations are worth making:

- The apparent protection of commercial and industrial users may explain why the changes in wages and salaries were much smaller than the change in water use. Commercial and industrial cutbacks that would have affected wages, salaries, and profits may have been largely avoided.

- The large drop in commercial and industrial use suggests that substantial reductions in commercial and industrial use were possible without major effects on wages and salaries. The effects on profits, however, still need to be explored.

Table 4.9

Percentage of Agencies Assessing Surcharges for Violations of Quantity Restrictions, by Customer Class
(N=14)

Customer Class	Percentage
Residential	93
Commercial	50
Industrial	36
Public authority	36

TYPE-OF-USE RESTRICTIONS

Overall Agency Strategy

A high proportion of the responding agencies adopted type-of-use restrictions at some time between 1986 and 1991. Examples included prohibitions on washing off driveways and sidewalks, irrigating during the day, and allowing sprinklers to run off into gutters. As shown in Table 4.4, between 65 and 77 percent of agencies adopted type-of-use restrictions. Most agencies adopted mandatory type-of-use restrictions. Panel A of Table 4.10 shows that type-of-use restrictions were mandatory in 72 percent of the agencies reporting type-of-use restrictions and that an additional 12 percent adopted a combination of mandatory and voluntary restrictions. Only 16 percent adopted completely voluntary restrictions.

Even though a sizable proportion of agencies adopted mandatory type-of-use restrictions, only a few actually levied fines. In most cases, the penalty for violating a mandatory type-of-use restriction was a fine that was not tied to water use. Penalties usually increased with each successive violation, culminating at least in principle in the installation of flow restrictors or termination of water service. Only 9 of the 46 agencies reporting mandatory type-of-use restriction (20 percent) assessed penalties.

Table 4.10

**Characteristics of Type-of-Use Restrictions,
Between 1986 and 1991
(N=55)**

	Percentage of Agencies with Type-of-Use Restrictions
A. Enforcement	
Mandatory only	72
Voluntary and mandatory	12
Voluntary only	16
B. Customer class targeted	
Single-dwelling unit	96
Multiple-dwelling unit	95
Commercial	95
Industrial	89

The fact that the few agencies that did levy penalties issued a sizable number of citations ironically provides indirect evidence that type-of-use restrictions were not well-enforced. Panel A of Table 4.11 shows that the number of penalties assessed was 12 percent of the number of accounts in agencies levying penalties that were able to report these data.[6] Twelve percent seems substantial, since in most cases the penalty involved writing up a citation at the site, rather than an automatic assessment through the billing system. Because type-of-use restrictions and penalties were similar across agencies, it seems unlikely that there would have been a significant number of violations in only a small percentage of agencies, as found here. This seems to suggest, therefore, that type-of-use restrictions were not well-enforced overall.

Even though type-of-use restrictions were apparently not well-enforced, consumers may still have been willing to pay a sizable amount to avoid them. Consumers may have obeyed the restrictions because of fears of penalties or social opprobrium even though the restrictions were not well-enforced. Information on how frequently consumers altered consumption patterns because of type-of-use restrictions would help to determine how widespread welfare losses were from type-of-use

Table 4.11

**Number of Penalties and Surcharges Assessed for
Type-of-Use Restrictions in 1991**

A. Number of penalties (N=8)	
Number assessed	68,716
Number of accounts	582,604
Ratio of number of penalties assessed to number of accounts	0.12
B. Fines assessed (N=5)	
Amount billed ($1000)	5,310
Number of penalties	68,674
Amount billed per penalty ($)	77.00

---

[6]Undoubtedly there were some repeat violators. How common these were, however, is not known.

restrictions during the drought.[7] The data presented here, however, do not provide strong evidence for substantial losses from type-of-use restrictions.

Variation by Customer Class

There is some evidence that agencies tried to protect commercial and industrial users from type-of-use restrictions. It is not as strong as the evidence for quantity restrictions, but given that type-of-use restrictions were not well-enforced overall, this is not surprising. Panel B of Table 4.10 shows that type-of-use restrictions were applied equally to all customer classes. In contrast, it appears that penalties for violating type-of-use restrictions were issued more frequently against residential users than against commercial and industrial users. All five agencies that were able to report type-of-use penalties by customer class assessed penalties against residential users, compared with only three against commercial users and two against industrial users. In summary, it appears that the already weak effect of type-of-use restrictions may have been further weakened for commercial and industrial users.

CONSERVATION PROGRAMS

As discussed in Section 2, voluntary conservation programs can reduce negative drought effects and can be categorized into two groups: education programs and device distribution programs. We first examine the education programs adopted during the drought.

Public Education Programs

Almost all agencies implemented some type of public education program between 1986 and 1991. Public education programs included bill inserts; television, radio, and newspaper announcements; school programs; and public displays. Seventy-three of the 76 agencies that answered the question on public education (96 percent) implemented some sort of public education program between 1986 and 1991. (See Table

---

[7]One might also try to estimate demand curves before and after the imposition of type-of-use restrictions and then calculate the change in consumer surplus.

4.4.) At 86 percent, even the lower bound on the percentage of agencies that implemented conservation programs remains high. Education programs for individual customers were far less common. Between 29 and 36 percent of the respondents conducted indoor or outdoor water audits for customers to help them identify how they could cut back water use. These education programs may have provided valuable information on how to reduce water use with little loss in welfare and, as explained in Section 2, altered how much individuals were willing to pay to avoid drought management programs.

Device Distribution Programs

A high percentage of agencies established device distribution programs. Between 76 and 87 percent of the responding agencies distributed conservation kits. (See Table 4.4.) These kits typically contained low-flow shower heads, toilet dams, and toilet leak detectors and were distributed free of charge. Between 27 and 32 percent of the responding agencies offered financial incentives for installing ULF toilets, which require no more than 1.6 gallons per flush. ULF toilet programs typically provided a $100 rebate to the customer for every ULF toilet installed.

Agencies spent considerable amounts on conservation programs. Table 4.12 shows the amount spent divided by the total number of accounts for agencies that could provide data on program expenditures. The most was spent per account on toilet rebates. Approximately $24 per account was spent on toilet rebates compared with $6 and $4 per account on public education and conservation kits, respectively. Relatively little was spent per account on water audits.[8] Even though a much smaller proportion of agencies had toilet rebate programs, the amounts spent per account shown in Table 4.12 suggest that, across all agencies, the total amount spent on toilet rebates was higher than for other

-----

[8]The results in Table 4.12 and 4.13 can be combined to determine the cost of conservation programs per unit. In the case of ULF toilets, $23.54 was spent per account and 0.261 rebates were issued per account. The cost per rebate was approximately $90 ($23.54/0.261). Conservation kits were approximately $14 per unit and water audits were approximately $62 per unit.

Table 4.12

Expenditures on Conservation Programs, 1986-1991

	Number Engaged in Activity	Number of Agencies Reporting	Amount Spent ($1,000)	Number of Accounts (1,000s)	Dollars/ Account
Public education	73	56	15,232	2,740	5.56
Audits	25	7	2,696	1,605	1.67
Conservation kits	65	47	10,782	2,420	4.45
ULF toilet rebates	23	19	22,924	974	23.54

conservation programs. The low amount spent per account and the relatively low proportion of agencies that offered audits suggest the least was spent on audits.[9]

Water agencies reached a considerable number of their customers with conservation programs during the drought. Table 4.13 shows that nearly 753,000 conservation kits were distributed in 59 of the 65 agencies that distributed conservation kits. This comes to nearly one-third of the total number of accounts. Similarly, ULF toilet rebates totaled 26 percent of the number of accounts in 10 of the 23 agencies that issued toilet rebates. These figures suggest that conservation programs may well have reduced the impact of the drought on water users.

The number of conservation kits, toilet rebates, and audits per account also illustrate how much more could be done to mitigate the effects of quantity restrictions. Not only could the agencies with conservation programs reach a substantial number of additional customers,[10] but a substantial share of agencies did not adopt some programs. For example, less than a third of agencies adopted toilet rebate programs. Whether agencies should continue to push these

---

[9]As a rough approximation of the total amount spent by the responding agencies on each program, the amount spent for the reporting agencies (column 3 in Table 4.12) is scaled up to the number of agencies engaged in the activity (column 1).

[10]Individual customers may receive more than one conservation kit or ULF toilet rebate. Thus the percentage of customers reached may be lower than the ratios in Table 4.13.

Table 4.13

**Conservation Program Activity Per Account for Agencies Reporting
Conservation Activity and Number of Accounts**

	Number of Agencies[a]	Number Performed or Issued	Number of Agencies[a]	Number Performed or Issued Per Account
Public education	73	NA	NA	NA
Audits				
Residential	25	46,472	22	0.026
Commercial	25	5,674	19	0.036
Industrial	25	94	12	0.004
Public authority	25	126	16	0.006
Total	25	52,366	24	0.027
Conservation kits				
Residential	59	733,194	48	0.223
Commercial	59	19,315	44	0.046
Industrial	59	380	34	0.002
Total	59	752,889	59	0.315
ULF toilet rebates				
Residential	10	192,172	7	0.272
Commercial	10	9,296	7	0.126
Industrial	10	10	6	0.001
Public authority	10	0	5	0
Total	10	201,478	10	0.261

[a]Number of agencies upon which data are based.

programs from a societal perspective depends on the overall program
benefits and costs.

Variation by Customer Class

It appears that conservation programs were targeted mainly at
residential customers. Table 4.13 shows that the vast majority of
conservation kits, water audits, and ULF toilet rebates went to
residential users. Information on how agencies targeted public
education programs was not readily available. Even when adjusted for
the number of accounts in each customer class, residential users
benefited disproportionately. For agencies that issued conservation
kits, 0.22 kits were issued per residential account versus 0.05 per
commercial account, and a negligible number per industrial account. The
numbers are similarly skewed for ULF toilet rebates. The number of

water audits per customer class is more uniform across customer classes, but the number of audits per account was very low.

Agencies may have focused conservation kits, water audits, and ULF toilet rebates on residential users because they thought that their drought management programs had the greatest impact on residential users. Water agencies may also have assumed that commercial and industrial users had the resources and expertise to purchase conservation devices themselves.[11] For example, commercial and industrial users may have facilities managers who are explicitly tasked to reduce water costs. Additional data are necessary to determine if commercial and industrial users installed conservation devices independently of agency programs.

PRICE CHANGES

Overall Agency Strategy

Price increases may have been a major source of loss to consumers during the drought. Increasing prices will decrease the net benefit of consuming a given amount of water as well as reduce the amount consumed, further decreasing net benefits of water use. We find evidence that agencies increased water prices during the drought with consequent negative effects on consumers. Some of these changes would have happened had there been no drought, for example, due to increasingly strict drinking-water standards. Others may be directly attributed to the drought, for example, due to higher water purchase costs, lower water sales, or the costs of device distribution and conservation programs.

As discussed above, penalties for violations of quantity restrictions in effect created an increasing block rate pricing structure. Many agencies also changed their pricing practices independent of quantity penalties. These changes were sometimes made to encourage conservation and sometimes to maintain revenues in the face

---

[11]Also, the low-cost conservation devices commonly distributed to households, such as low-flow showerheads and toilet bags or dams, are frequently not relevant to business users. Businesses often have few or no showers and have flushometer toilets instead of tank toilets.

of lower water sales.[12] Some agencies went from flat to increasing
block, and some reduced the fixed component of bills and increased the
variable costs. Survey respondents provided detailed information on how
their rate structures changed, but resources available to the project
did not allow analysis of these data. Further analysis would provide
valuable information on how consumers were affected by price changes.

We have been able, however, to analyze how average agency revenue
per unit of water delivered changed over the period.[13] Changes in
average revenue may either hide or exaggerate changes in price schedules
due to the drought. Average revenue may not change if an agency moves
to an increasing block rate structure but reduces fixed charges. In
contrast, increases in average revenue could simply reflect price
increases due to higher treatment costs rather than to limited supplies,
thus exaggerating the impact of the drought on price. In any case, it
is instructive to look at how average revenue changed during the drought
to gain some insight into how prices changed and which sectors were most
affected.

Average revenue per acre-foot rose 54 percent in nominal terms
between 1986 and 1991 for the 55 agencies providing data. (See Table
4.14.) When adjusted for inflation, average revenue per acre-foot rose
roughly 2 percent in 1989 and 4 percent in 1990, and then rose
approximately 12 percent in 1991. The large jump in 1991 suggests that
agency responses to the drought did cause large increases in price and
that the observed price changes were not caused by secular trends in
water treatment costs.

Table 4.15 reports how changes in average revenue varied by region,
agency size, and customer class. Of the three regions, average revenue
grew fastest in Southern California between 1986 and 1990 and in the Bay
Area between 1990 and 1991. Average revenue grew faster in the larger
agencies in the earlier years, but there was little difference in the

---

[12] Reduced water sales reduce agency variable costs, but not fixed
costs. Thus, lower water sales may force agencies to increase water
prices to continue to cover their fixed costs.

[13] Average revenue per unit of water is calculated by dividing total
agency revenue by water deliveries. Income from drought penalties and
surcharges is included.

Table 4.14

Average Agency Revenue Per Acre-Foot
(N=55)

	Total Water Use (millions of acre-feet)	Total Water Revenue (millions of dollars)	Average Revenue (dollars per acre-foot)	Annual Percentage Change	
				Average Revenue	Real Average Revenue[a]
1986	2.09	795	381	---	---
1987	2.14	849	397	4.2	0
1988	2.11	906	430	8.3	3.7
1989	2.13	983	462	7.4	2.3
1990	2.12	1,069	505	9.3	4.0
1991	1.83	1,072	585	15.8	12.3

[a]Real average revenue calculated using consumer price index for California.

Table 4.15

Average Water Revenue by Region, Agency Size, and Customer Class

	N	($/acre-foot)						Percentage Change	
		1986	1987	1988	1989	1990	1991	1986-1990	1990-1991
All	55	381	397	430	462	505	585	33	16
Region									
Bay Area	11	409	405	471	476	514	683	26	33
So. Calif.	30	385	408	436	484	529	576	37	9
Rest of state	14	299	324	318	323	368	451	23	23
Agency population (thousands)									
10-50	14	437	440	448	471	491	560	12	14
51-100	20	410	423	440	470	523	610	28	17
>100	21	374	391	427	460	504	582	35	15
Customer class									
Residential	34	404	421	449	490	543	619	34	14
Commercial	31	378	395	453	496	533	618	41	16
Industrial	28	336	352	422	433	466	567	39	22
Agricultural	8	275	278	301	336	340	329	24	-3

change in average revenue between 1990 and 1991 by agency size. Statistical analysis would be needed to determine whether the difference in average revenue growth is correlated with agency size or location.

Variation by Customer Class

Average revenue per acre-foot grew faster for commercial and industrial water sales than for residential sales both between 1986 and 1990 and between 1990 and 1991.[14] These higher growth rates brought commercial and industrial average revenues closer to residential average revenue.

The difference in growth rates may be due to several factors. It may reflect rapid movement away from decreasing block rates for commercial and industrial users, something that largely had already happened for residential users. It may be that fixed charges account for a lower portion of industrial user bills so that comparable increases in the variable charge for all customer classes result in a greater percentage increase in average cost for industrial customers.

It is unclear how much of the difference in growth rates was due to the drought. It may be that agencies would have attempted to narrow differences in average revenues across customer classes even if there had been no drought. In any case, the relatively rapid growth in commercial and industrial average revenue suggests, in contrast to previous findings in this section, that commercial and industrial users were not shielded from price increases as a drought management strategy.

Average revenues per acre-foot for agriculture grew far more slowly than those for other customer classes between 1986 and 1990 and actually fell between 1990 and 1991. What is more, the 1986 average revenue for agriculture was substantially lower than for those in the other classes. These lower costs and growth rates may be because agricultural water is not treated to the same standards as water delivered to other customer classes or because agricultural service is often interruptible. Many

---

[14] Since the number of agencies responding varies by customer class, care must be taken in interpreting differences in average revenue across customer classes. The same holds for growth rates in average revenue across customer classes over time, but the problem may be less significant.

urban water agencies do not have separate distribution systems for agricultural customers, however, so these findings may also suggest that agricultural users were treated favorably both before and during the drought.

Findings on changes in average revenue per acre-foot suggest that all sectors, with the exception of agriculture, were adversely affected by price changes caused by the drought.

SUPPLY AUGMENTATION STRATEGIES

More than half of the agencies responding to the survey received supplies from the 1991 Drought Water Bank run by the California Department of Water Resources. (A list of the urban agencies receiving water from the water bank and the amounts received is included as Appendix C.)[15] These supplies reduced drought effects from what they would have been otherwise.

Water received from the water bank amounted to 5.3 percent of total 1991 water use in the 77 responding agencies that were able to provide data on water use. (See Table 4.16.) Water bank supplies ranged from less than 0.5 percent to 40 percent of 1991 water use in the 43 responding agencies that received water bank supplies, and nearly 10 percent of the combined 1991 water use in these districts was received from the water bank. These percentages suggest that the water bank generated sizable benefits in many urban areas.

Based on responses to the survey, 59 percent of the agencies receiving bank water had no alternate supplies. This suggests that in these agencies, water use would have dropped even more than it did in 1991 had there been no water bank. As reported in Section 2, per-capita water use fell approximately 18 percent in the responding agencies between 1990 and 1991. This drop may have been 10 percentage points

---

[15] Many retail agencies were not aware that they had received water from the Drought Water Bank because bank water was purchased by wholesale agencies and commingled with other water supplies before it was passed on to the retail agencies. We contacted the purchasers of 1991 Drought Water Bank water and, in the case of the Metropolitan Water District of Southern California, another layer of wholesale agencies, to determine how bank supplies were allocated to retail water agencies. See Appendix C for details.

Table 4.16

1991 Water Bank Purchases

	Thousands of Acre-Feet		
	1991 Usage	Water Bank Purchases	Percentage of Total
All respondents providing water use data (N=77)	2,760	147	5.3
All respondents providing water use data and receiving water-bank water (N=43)	1,546	147	9.5

larger in agencies with no alternative water supplies. The remaining 41 percent of agencies reported having access to alternative water supplies. Presumably, these supplies were more expensive than those from the water bank or were insurance against a sixth year of drought, and therefore, consumers in these districts were also better off as a result of the water bank's operation.

Agencies receiving water-bank supplies were asked how their drought management strategies would have changed had there been no water bank. Their responses provide further evidence that the water bank benefited urban consumers. As shown in Table 4.17, almost all the agencies that received bank water and answered the question said they would have tightened quantity restrictions had there been no water bank. Sixty percent would have strengthened type-of-use restrictions, and one-third would have increased prices. Agencies would also have tried to reduce water use by expanding conservation programs, with increased public education the most frequently mentioned.

SUMMARY

Investigation of drought management strategies suggests that the drought had widespread negative effects in urban areas, with the principal effects in 1991. The main source of losses appears to have been because of quantity restrictions that were usually coupled with price surcharges for use over a target amount. Evidence suggests that commercial and industrial users were shielded from the drought effects to some extent, although they appear to have suffered price increases much like the residential sector.

Table 4.17

**Drought Management Strategies That Would Have Been Modified
in the Absence of Water-Bank Water
(15 Respondents)**

Type of Policy	Percentage Indicating
Quantity restrictions	87
Public education	67
Type-of-use restrictions	60
Device distribution	33
Price increases	33
Water audits	20
Conservation rebates	13

Water agencies aggressively implemented device distribution, toilet rebate, and public education programs during the drought. These programs presumably reduced the drought's negative effects. Residential users were the main beneficiaries of these programs. This might be interpreted as evidence that residential users were hardest hit by the drought, leading agencies to focus attention on them.

Finally, the 1991 Drought Water Bank was an important source of water to many agencies. A majority of those receiving water had no alternative sources, which suggests that drought effects would have been considerably worse without the water bank.

5. PILOT STUDY OF RESIDENTIAL WELFARE LOSSES

In this section, we use demand curve analysis to estimate willingness-to-pay to avoid drought-related increases in water prices for a subset of customers in one part of California--households living in single-dwelling units in the Alameda County Water District (ACWD), an urban water district located on the southeast side of San Francisco Bay. This analysis provides an example of this method of estimating willingness-to-pay, illustrating both its advantages and disadvantages.

ACWD provided information on water use by 599 single-dwelling units over the period 1982-1992 that was used to extrapolate to approximately 54,000 single-dwelling units located in the ACWD service area, according to tax assessor records. Although we encountered some difficulties in estimating the relationship between water use and water prices under ACWD's steeply increasing block rate structure, we were able to construct two plausible sets of estimates for willingness-to-pay to avoid drought cutbacks.

We found that average residential welfare losses (for households living in single-dwelling units) due to drought-related price increases during the period from July 1991 to December 1992 were in the range of $14-$23 per household, or a total of $750,000 to $1,270,000 for the entire district. We discuss below the factors that may cause these estimates to overstate or understate the actual willingness-to-pay to avoid all of the drought management policies adopted by ACWD.

In the subsections below, we describe the data used in our analysis, the statistical techniques used to estimate the demand relationships, and the resulting estimates. We then use these estimates to calculate consumer surplus losses due to the price increases in ACWD during the drought, for households living in single-dwelling units.

DESCRIPTION OF ACWD DATA

Our data on water use come from ACWD, which covers Fremont, Newark, and Union City, California, in the Southeast San Francisco Bay Area, south of Oakland. ACWD used a steeply increasing block rate structure as one of its drought management policies, which enables us to estimate water demand relationships at high price levels. It also had a uniquely comprehensive data set that covered water use by nearly 600 households over a 10-year period, including the drought.[1] As of 1991, ACWD served a population of about 270,000, with 69,000 customer accounts. ACWD's records indicate that approximately 63,000 are single-dwelling unit accounts,[2] 2,200 multiple-dwelling unit (e.g., apartment buildings), 2,400 commercial, 400 industrial, and 1,000 public authority accounts.[3]

The data used for our analysis were collected for a water demand forecast conducted by Brown and Caldwell Consultants [1992] for ACWD. Bimonthly meter readings for a sample of 599 single-dwelling units were collected from January 1982 through July 1992. Clusters of households in various parts of the district were sampled.[4] These data were matched with the ACWD price schedule; monthly precipitation and maximum, minimum, and average temperatures from the National Oceanic and Atmospheric Administration weather station in Newark, CA; and Alameda County tax assessor data. In addition, we obtained 1980 and 1990 census data regarding household size and composition, median incomes, etc., at the block group level for the census tracts corresponding to the ACWD service area,[5] and information on ACWD's drought management policies through the survey of urban water agencies described in this report.

------

[1]Most water agencies only retain 1-2 years of billing records in electronic format. Part of the data collected by ACWD for the Brown and Caldwell [1992] demand analysis had to be retrieved from archived paper records.

[2]The discrepancy between the number of single-dwelling units in the tax assessor data and in ACWD's records is discussed below.

[3]This information was obtained from ACWD's response to the water agency survey described in the previous sections.

[4]The sample was drawn by Brown and Caldwell based on street blocks. Households located on a total of 20 blocks were chosen to reflect each city's population: 13 blocks (65%) from Fremont, 4 blocks (20%) from Union City, and 3 blocks (15%) from Newark. The blocks were also chosen to be evenly distributed across the ACWD service area, including some blocks in the eastern hills, and to reflect the distribution of property values for the entire ACWD area. See Brown and Caldwell [1992], pp. 2-11 to 2-12.

[5]A block group is a subdivision of a census tract, generally containing between 250 and 550 housing units, with a target size of 400 housing units. Block groups provide more disaggregated data than tracts, which usually contain between 2,500 and 8,000 persons.

ACWD's commodity charges for water over the period 1982-1992 are shown in Table 5.1. The nominal water price was raised infrequently during the early to mid-1980s, so prices were falling in real terms for some years.[6] As the drought began in the late 1980s, nominal prices were raised each year, and except for 1990, there was also a real price increase. In July 1991, ACWD introduced a steeply increasing block rate structure as a drought management policy. The base allowance per single-dwelling unit was 28 CCF (28 hundred cubic feet) per bimonthly billing period, or approximately 350 gallons per day.[7] If consumption stayed within the base allowance, households paid the flat rate price that had been in effect before the rate change. At higher levels of use, the water price was doubled, tripled, and quadrupled. The price for the base allowance was increased in January 1992, but the rest of the rate structure remained the same. In July 1992, the single-dwelling unit allowance was increased to 30 CCF per bimonthly period, or approximately 400 gallons per day, and the rate of price increase over the higher blocks became less steep.

ACWD also implemented other drought management policies aimed at reducing water use by households in single-dwelling units. A public education program including bill inserts, newspaper ads, school programs, and public displays began in 1986. Conservation kits were distributed beginning in 1989. Restrictions on types of water use were in effect from May 1, 1991, to April 1, 1993. These restrictions included prohibitions on using water in an irresponsible manner that results in wastage, watering landscape in a manner that results in flooding or runoff, using hoses to clean hard surfaces, and use of a hose for any purpose without a shutoff nozzle. Households could also appeal to obtain more than the bimonthly 28 CCF allowance at the lowest

---

[6]Nominal water prices were converted to 1992 real prices using the Consumer Price Index for the western United States. See Brown and Caldwell [1992], Appendix B.

[7]One hundred cubic feet of water is equivalent to approximately 750 gallons. Average household water use per billing period for the 600-household sample was 27 CCF, so the baseline was approximately equal to average use. (See Table 5.2 below.)

block price if there were more than four household members. Ideally, the estimation of household water demand curves should take these other

Table 5.1

ACWD Residential Water Prices for Single-Dwelling Units

Effective Date	Usage Level (per billing period)	Nominal Price Per CCF	Real Price Per CCF (1992=100)
January 1, 1982	All	$0.450	$0.6616
May 1, 1982	All	0.585	0.8550
January 1, 1983	All	0.585	0.8384
January 1, 1984	All	0.585	0.8114
July 1, 1984	All	0.673	0.9147
January 1, 1985	All	0.673	0.8843
January 1, 1986	All	0.673	0.8642
January 1, 1987	All	0.740	0.9187
January 1, 1988	All	0.777	0.9266
January 1, 1989	All	0.816	0.9292
January 1, 1990	All	0.857	0.9247
January 1, 1991	All	0.900	0.9349
July 1, 1991	0-28 CCF	0.900	0.9221
	29-38 CCF	1.800	1.8442
	39-48 CCF	2.700	2.7664
	>48 CCF	3.600	3.6883
January 1, 1992	0-28 CCF	1.008	1.0144
	29-38 CCF	1.800	1.8115
	39-48 CCF	2.700	2.7172
	>48 CCF	3.600	3.6223
July 1, 1992	0-30 CCF	1.008	1.0080
	31-48 CCF	1.260	1.2600
	49-64 CCF	1.512	1.5120
	65-80 CCF	1.764	1.7640
	>80 CCF	2.016	2.0160

SOURCE: Brown and Caldwell [1992] and Alameda County Water District.
NOTE: CCF = one hundred cubic feet.

policies into account. We show the effects of including drought management policy variables in the ordinary least squares (OLS) and fixed effects demand estimates below.

The Alameda County tax assessor data file originally consisted of 83,094 observations. Based on the use code, we eliminated all properties that were not single-dwelling units, resulting in a sample of 54,488 single-dwelling units.[8] There were six addresses in the sample of 599 households with water use data that did not match to the tax assessor data. These households were dropped from demand curve estimates that used house size and lot size as regressors. The tax assessor data also serve as a basis of extrapolation to determine predicted demand and consumer surplus losses for all single-dwelling units in the ACWD service area.

Both the small sample of 599 addresses and the large sample of 54,488 addresses were matched to census block groups using the geographical information system ARC/INFO.[9] The median or average values of census variables (depending on the type of variable) for the block group were assigned to each household located in the block group. Census variables potentially affecting household water use include median household income, per-capita income, number of persons per household, poverty status, employment status, number of rooms or bathrooms per house, and median owner costs with and without mortgage.[10]

_____

[8]It is not clear whether the discrepancy between the 54,000 observations in the tax assessor data and the 63,000 single-dwelling unit accounts reported by ACWD is due to multiple accounts at the same household, incorrect categorization of accounts by customer type, or incorrect codes in the tax assessor file. We base our extrapolation on the 54,000 households in the tax assessor file because the extrapolation depends on the house size and lot size of each single-dwelling unit.

[9]All of the 599 addresses in the ACWD file were successfully matched to the census data, but there were about 7,500 nonmatching addresses in the tax assessor file. Since the census variables did not prove to be significant in the water demand estimates, we did not undertake further efforts to match the addresses to the census block groups by hand.

[10]Census variables could also form the basis of an analysis of correlations between block group characteristics and drought-related consumer surplus losses. For example, one could examine whether drought management policies had a greater impact on high or low income groups by matching predicted average household losses in each block group with the

Table 5.2

Descriptive Statistics for Variables Used in Estimations

Variable	Mean	Standard Deviation	Minimum Value	Maximum Value
Bimonthly water use (CCF)	27.05	16.78	0	190
House size (1000s of sq. ft.)	1.49	0.38	0.53	2.89
Lot size (1000s of sq. ft.)	6.65	1.48	4.69	17.29
Precipitation (inches in billing month)	1.15	1.43	0	7.17
Lagged precipitation (inches in previous month)	1.25	1.62	0	7.17
Average temperature (°F in billing month)	59.65	6.80	44	74
Lagged average temperature (°F in previous month)	59.46	7.00	44	74
Price (1992 $ per CCF)	0.93	0.26	0.66	3.69
Price^2	0.93	0.99	0.44	13.60
Public education (dummy variable)	0.63	0.48	0	1
Conservation kits (dummy variable)	0.34	0.47	0	1
Type-of-use restrictions (dummy variable)	0.12	0.32	0	1

NOTE: Dummy variables take on a value of one when the policy is in effect and zero when the policy is not in effect. They therefore increase or decrease the constant term in the demand equation by the estimated value of the coefficient.

Means, standard deviations, and minimum and maximum values for each of the variables used in the estimates reported below are shown in Table 5.2.

DEMAND CURVE ESTIMATES

We estimated new water demand curves because most past estimates of household water demand are based on relatively small variation in the

median income for the block group. A steeply increasing block rate structure is likely to impose higher costs on high-use households, which could be correlated either with high income or with a large number of persons per household, and thus with low income.

price of water during nondrought periods. Much wider variations in price structures and household water use were observed during the California drought.[11] Thus, extrapolations from existing studies of water demand during nondrought periods are likely to produce unreliable estimates of household behavior and resulting welfare losses during the drought.[12] In addition, ACWD adopted a steeply increasing block rate structure, and most currently existing demand relationships are not structured to predict the effects of changing block rate structures on consumption.

We show the results of three different approaches to estimating demand curves: OLS, fixed effects, and maximum likelihood. We made preliminary estimates of household water demand as a function of house size, lot size, weather variables, census variables, and drought management policies using OLS regression. The increasing block rate structure that was in effect from July 1991 through July 1992 created a positive correlation between high levels of use and high prices during those billing periods. As a result, the OLS estimates yielded demand curves that slope downward at low price levels but began to slope upward at high price levels.

Although one would expect that OLS regression would not deal well with the correlation between high prices and high water use, it was a fairly standard approach in some of the previous literature on water demand. Corrections for block rate structure effects tended to take the form of including a measure of the difference between the household's actual bill and the bill it would have paid if all water had been purchased at the marginal price (Billings and Agthe [1980]), or

---

[11] The real price increase at ACWD was almost 450 percent from the 1982 flat rate to the highest block rate in 1991. In contrast, the real price increase in the mean-use block in Tucson, Arizona, one of the most heavily studied cities, was only 12 percent between 1974 and 1977. (See Martin et al. [1984].) Nieswiadomy and Molina's [1989] data set for Denton, Texas showed a real price increase of 107 percent for the highest block rate between 1977 and 1985.

[12] Nor is it feasible to predict customer responses to the block rate structure implemented by ACWD based on pre-1991 demand. Prior to July 1991, real prices ranged only from $0.66 to $0.93 per CCF. OLS and fixed effects estimates of demand curves based on the pre-1991 period predict negative water use at prices above $1.25 to $1.50 per CCF.

predicting which block the customer would choose using two-stage least squares or instrumental variables (Nieswiadomy and Molina [1989]). Based on the OLS results for the ACWD data shown below, it appears that the lack of price variation in some of the data sets used by these authors masked more fundamental problems with the econometric techniques being used.

Therefore, we employed more sophisticated econometric techniques designed to control for unobserved differences between households and to model consumer response to block rate structures. The OLS estimates do not control for household differences, because they treat each bimonthly meter reading as an independent observation and do not take advantage of the availability of multiple observations from the same households. One technique that uses the panel data set to control for household differences is a fixed effects model, which essentially allows each household to have a different constant term in the regression equation. A fixed effects model could correct for the endogeneity of prices at observed consumption levels if high-use households were cutting back relative to their normal use in nondrought periods. Thus, each household would have a downward-sloping demand for water, but high-use households would have a higher constant term. In practice, the fixed effects technique improved the explanatory power of the independent variables, but it still resulted in demand curves that sloped upward at high prices because of the increasing block rate structure.

To model customer responses to the block rate structure, we used a maximum likelihood approach based on previous work by Hewitt [1993]. We estimated three versions of Hewitt's model, which vary based on assumptions about error structure of the model. These models potentially correct for the endogeneity of prices at observed consumption levels by jointly estimating the probability that the household is in a particular block of the rate structure, and the conditional probability of the level of use, given the probability that the household chose that block. Estimating errors might occur either because the researcher cannot observe all of the characteristics that influence household water use, or because the household cannot accurately monitor or control its use, so that observed water use differs from the household's intended water use. Either type of error could cause observed water use to be unusually high in some periods, even though the household did (or intended to) cut back water use in response to the increasing block rate structure. As we show below, two versions of the maximum likelihood model yielded downward-sloping demand curves that could be used as a basis to estimate consumer surplus losses during the drought.

We discuss the OLS, fixed effects, and maximum likelihood estimates of household water demand in the paragraphs below.

Ordinary Least Squares Models

We conducted a preliminary analysis of the data using OLS estimates of simple demand curve specifications based on water prices, house size, lot size, weather, and census variables. We present the results of the best-fitting models in this section to illustrate the endogeneity problem, and for comparison with past estimates of water demand. Model 1 estimates the effects of price changes on water use without controlling for the use of other drought management policies. Dummy variables for other drought management policies are successively introduced in Models 2-4. Model 2 adds a variable indicating when public education programs were in effect; Model 3 adds a variable indicating when conservation kits were being distributed; and Model 4 adds a variable indicating when type-of-use restrictions were in effect. The four model types are summarized in Table 5.3. The equation for Model 1 is given by:

$$\text{Water Use} = \text{Constant} + \beta_1 \text{House Size} + \beta_2 \text{Lot Size} + \beta_3 \text{Precipitation}$$
$$+ \beta_4 \text{Lagged Precipitation} + \beta_5 \text{Temperature} + \beta_6 \text{Lagged Temperature}$$
$$+ \beta_7 \text{Price} + \beta_8 \text{Price}^2 .$$

As shown in Table 5.3, additional terms for the drought management policy variables are added to Models 2-4.

The estimated coefficients for Models 1-4 are shown in Table 5.4. The t-statistics indicate that all coefficients are significant at the 0.01 confidence level or higher.[13] Both house size and lot size are

---

[13] In other words, the probability that the true coefficient is zero is .01 or lower.

Table 5.3

Model Specification--Drought Management Policies

Model	Policies Analyzed	Period When Policy Was in Effect
Model 1	Water price	All periods
Model 2	Water price	All periods
	Public education	1/86 to end of sample
Model 3	Water price	All periods
	Public education	1/86 to end of sample
	Conservation kits	1/89 to end of sample
Model 4	Water price	All periods
	Public education	1/86 to end of sample
	Conservation kits	1/89 to end of sample
	Type-of-use restrictions	5/91 to end of sample

NOTE: The sample period ends in July 1992. Some drought management policies remained in effect after this period.

highly significant in explaining bimonthly water use, as are the current and lagged monthly precipitation and average temperature.[14] However, the increasing block rate structure in effect during the drought creates a correlation between the highest price levels and the highest levels of water use. Therefore, these demand curves become upward sloping at higher prices for Models 1-3 and at all prices for Model 4.[15] Another shortcoming of these simple OLS models is that they only explain 25-30 percent of the variance in household water use.

As expected, the drought management policy variables shift the demand curves to the left (i.e., they reduce demand at each price level), but because they were in effect during overlapping periods, and at the same time as the increasing block rate price structure, they change the slope of the demand curve and tend to reduce the significance

---

[14] Since each water bill covers a two-month period, we use weather variables representing the current month and the previous month.

[15] Because the coefficient on the squared price is positive, the demand curve must eventually slope upward as the price increases. The problem here is that water use begins to increase before the maximum block rate of $3.60 is reached. This occurs because high water users are charged a higher price, not because high prices cause consumers to use more water.

Table 5.4

Estimated OLS Coefficients and t-Statistics
(Dependent Variable: Bimonthly Water Use in CCF)

Variable	Model 1	Model 2	Model 3	Model 4
Constant	-32.353	-32.565	-35.135	-46.499
(t statistic)	(-22.19)	(-22.39)	(-24.22)	(-30.93)
House size	0.0064	0.0064	0.0064	0.0064
(sq. ft.)	(28.56)	(28.51)	(28.59)	(28.74)
Lot size	0.0011	0.0011	0.0011	0.0011
(sq. ft.)	(19.62)	(19.58)	(19.63)	(19.68)
Precipitation	-0.3524	-0.4958	-0.5574	-0.3447
(inches per month)	(-5.14)	(-7.18)	(-8.11)	(-5.03)
Lagged	-1.0039	-1.1742	-1.1863	-1.1470
precipitation	(-16.72)	(-19.24)	(-19.55)	(-19.07)
Monthly average	0.2865	0.2714	0.2583	0.3021
temperature (°F)	(14.94)	(14.17)	(13.56)	(15.94)
Lagged average	0.6483	0.6001	0.5622	0.5562
temperature	(34.95)	(31.91)	(29.94)	(29.89)
Price	-19.244	-10.705	-2.3095	10.083
(1992 $ per CCF)	(-13.81)	(-7.08)	(-1.49)	(6.25)
Price^2	6.7308	4.7572	2.9875	0.6467
	(18.34)	(12.16)	(7.51)	(1.60)
Public education		-2.6509	-0.9569	-1.2959
		(-14.30)	(-4.77)	(-6.50)
Conservation kits			-4.2934	-2.2570
			(-21.23)	(-10.48)
Type-of-use				-7.6972
restrictions				(-25.84)
Adjusted R^2	0.2533	0.2574	0.2665	0.2796

NOTE: During periods when the block rate structure was in effect, the price variable was set equal to marginal price at observed use.

of the other policy variables and of the price variables. It appears to be impossible to separate the effects of price and other drought management policies using a simple OLS model. In contrast, the coefficients of the house size, lot size, and weather variables are relatively stable as the drought management policy variables are introduced.

The estimated demand curves in Models 1-4 are evaluated at median house size and lot size and average winter and summer precipitation and temperatures and graphed in Figures 5.1-5.4. This clearly illustrates the problem of upward-sloping demand and the effect of successively introducing the drought management policy variables. The drought management variables appear to account for more and more of the change in water use, while the slope of the demand curve more closely reflects the steep block rate structure. Estimated price elasticities on the downward-sloping portions of these curves are relatively low. The highest point elasticity on the Model 1 winter demand curve is -0.33 at a price of 82 cents per CCF, and on the summer demand curve, -0.20 at a price of 78 cents per CCF.

Census variables were not included in the models presented here because these variables resulted in coefficients that were insignificant and/or had the wrong sign. Median household income, for example, was positively correlated with house size and lot size, and often had a

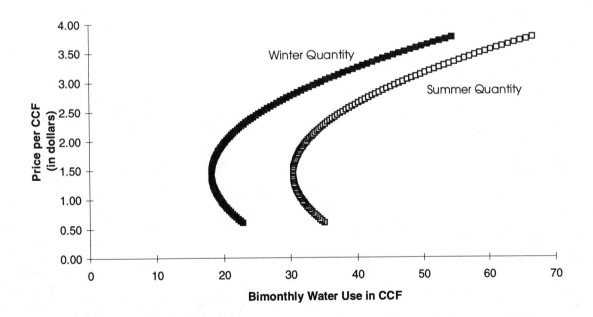

Figure 5.1--Winter and Summer Demand Curves Based on OLS Model 1

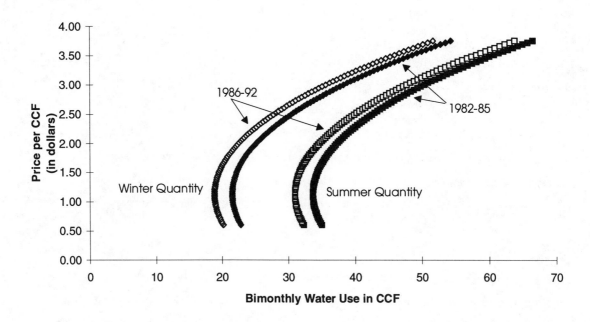

Figure 5.2--Winter and Summer Demand Curves Based on OLS Model 2

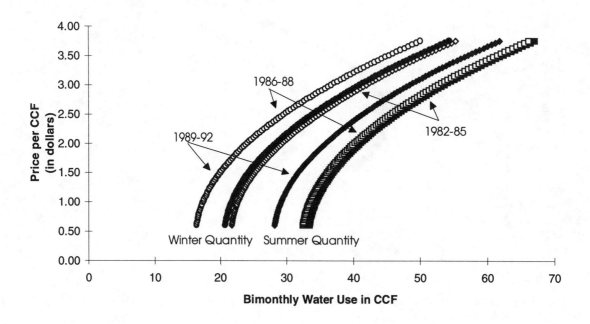

Figure 5.3--Winter and Summer Demand Curves Based on OLS Model 3

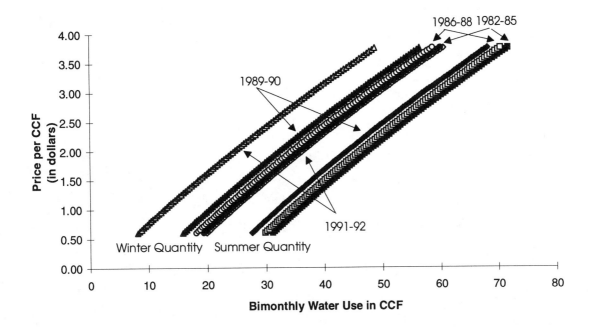

Figure 5.4--Winter and Summer Demand Curves Based on OLS Model 4

negative sign when all three variables were employed.[16] It also tended
to be less significant because of the greater measurement error involved
in linking households with the median income for their block group
rather than actual household income.[17]

Because of the endogeneity of price at the observed consumption
level, the OLS estimates did not yield reasonable water demand curves.
In the paragraphs below, we show estimates of the fixed effects and
maximum likelihood models, which have the potential to correct for the
endogeneity of price.

Fixed Effects Models

Fixed effects models estimate household water use as a deviation
from the household's average use, based on the deviations of the

---

[16]Strong correlations between the explanatory variables in a
regression cause their coefficients to be imprecisely estimated.
Although the combined effects of the correlated variables may be
correctly estimated, the coefficient estimates for the individual
variables are unreliable.

[17]The census variables were also tested in the fixed effects
models, but not in the maximum likelihood models because of the large
amount of computational time needed to estimate each model.

explanatory variables from their averages. The OLS regression models discussed above had the form:

Water Use = Constant + β_1House Size + β_2Lot Size + β_3Precipitation + β_4Lagged Precipitation + β_5Temperature + β_6Lagged Temperature + β_7Price + β_8Price^2.

The analogous fixed effects model has the form:

Water Use - Avg. Water Use = (Constant - Avg. Constant) + β_1(House Size - Avg. House Size) + β_2(Lot Size - Avg. Lot Size) + β_3(Precipitation - Avg. Precipitation) + β_4(Lagged Precipitation - Avg. Lagged Precipitation) + β_5(Temperature - Avg. Temperature) + β_6(Lagged Temperature - Avg. Lagged Temperature) + β_7(Price - Avg. Price) + β_8(Price^2 - Avg. (Price^2)).

Since the constant, house size, and lot size do not change over the sample period for an individual household, the first three terms in this equation equal zero. Thus, rearranging terms, we have:

Water Use = Avg. Water Use + β_3(Precipitation - Avg. Precipitation) + β_4(Lagged Precipitation - Avg. Lagged Precipitation) + β_5(Temperature - Avg. Temperature) + β_6(Lagged Temperature - Avg. Lagged Temperature) + β_7(Price - Avg. Price) + β_8(Price^2 - Avg. (Price^2)).

This technique therefore allows each household's demand curve to have its own constant term, based on the household's average water use over the sample period.[18] The estimated coefficients represent the impact of changes in weather or price on household water use. So, for example, if the coefficient β_5 is positive, household water use is predicted to be above average when the temperature is above average.

This approach could solve the endogeneity problem observed in the OLS estimates if the high-use households who paid the highest block rates during the drought were cutting back relative to their normal use in nondrought periods. Thus, each household could actually have a downward-sloping demand for water, but higher-use households would have

---

[18]This constant term represents observable or unobservable characteristics that do not change over time. Thus, the household constant term includes effects due to observable variables, such as house size and lot size, as well as unobservable variables, such as whether the household has a swimming pool or a sprinkler system.

a higher constant term. However, this hypothesis was not borne out in the fixed effects estimates, shown in Table 5.5. (Models 1-4 are equivalent to the OLS models shown above.) Although the household-specific constants approximately double the explanatory power of the equations from roughly 25 percent to 50 percent of the variance in water use, the fixed effects models still result in upward-sloping demand at high prices because of the correlation between high use and high price. Winter and summer demand curves estimated with fixed effects Model 1 are shown for illustration in Figure 5.5.

The problem of upward-sloping demand may be persisting in the fixed effects model because the temperature and precipitation variables do not adequately control for seasonal fluctuations in water use, which appear to be more important predictors than price. Figure 5.6 shows an example of water use, temperature, and precipitation patterns for one of the 600 households, chosen because it occasionally had high water use during the drought. The figure illustrates that households do not generally have consistently high use, but only occasional high use during the hot, dry summer months. If the fixed effects model is not accurately capturing the effect of seasonal variables on water use, then the households' response to water price may be incorrectly estimated.

Maximum Likelihood Models

The third approach that we employed to estimate water demand was maximum likelihood models. These models are based on likelihood functions that reflect the probability that a household chose a particular block in the block rate structure, combined with the probability of its particular level of use, given the block that was chosen. We estimated three different maximum likelihood models, based on previous work by Hewitt [1993]: the heterogeneous preferences model, the error perception model, and the two-error model. The structure of each model is based on the assumed source of the error in estimating household demand, such as errors in the data, missing variables, or

Table 5.5

Estimated Fixed Effects Coefficients and t-Statistics
(Dependent Variable: Bimonthly Water Use in CCF)

Variable	Model 1	Model 2	Model 3	Model 4
Precipitation (t statistic)	-0.3969 (-7.19)	-0.5104 (-9.17)	-0.5625 (-10.17)	-0.3941 (-7.14)
Lagged precipitation	-1.0359 (-21.38)	-1.1696 (-23.75)	-1.1796 (-24.12)	-1.1470 (-23.66)
Average temperature	0.2960 (19.16)	0.2842 (18.42)	0.2730 (17.80)	0.3079 (20.18)
Lagged average temperature	0.6416 (42.94)	0.6032 (39.82)	0.5710 (37.78)	0.5656 (37.76)
Price	-22.745 (-20.18)	-15.909 (-13.00)	-8.7031 (-6.92)	1.4403 (1.10)
Price^2	6.6161 (22.22)	5.0361 (15.87)	3.5238 (10.93)	1.6215 (4.95)
Public education		-2.1178 (-14.16)	-0.6902 (-4.27)	-0.9663 (-6.02)
Conservation kits			-3.6398 (-22.36)	-2.0239 (-11.69)
Type-of-use restrictions				-6.1838 (-25.72)
R^2	.5223	.5250	.5314	.5398

NOTE: The constant term, house size, and lot size are absorbed into the household's individual intercept. During periods when the block rate structure was in effect, the price variable was set equal to marginal price at observed use.

errors in the household's actual consumption relative to its intended consumption.[19]

In the "heterogeneous preferences" model, the household's observed consumption is assumed to be equal to its intended consumption, but errors in estimation of demand arise because the researcher cannot observe all the relevant characteristics of the household. In the "error perception" model, the researcher is assumed to observe relevant

_____

[19] The maximum likelihood models presented here are described in greater detail in Appendix D.

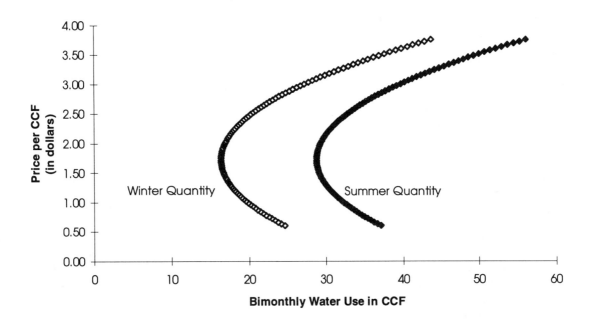

Figure 5.5--Winter and Summer Demand Curves Based on Fixed Effects Model 1

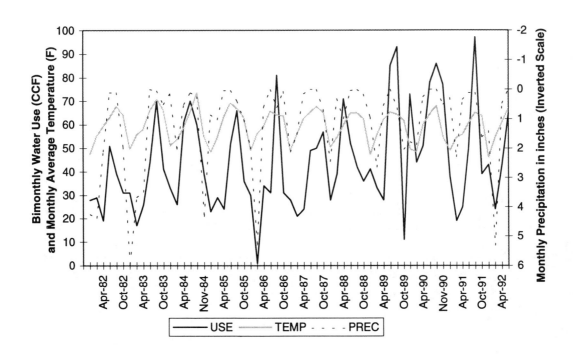

Figure 5.6--Seasonal Water Use by a High Use Household

household characteristics, but errors arise because the household's observed consumption is not necessarily equal to its intended consumption. For example, the household may make errors in consumption because it is difficult to monitor and control water use by all household members during the billing period. The "two-error" model combines both sources of error and is therefore more general than the other two, but it is also more complex to estimate. These three model specifications are summarized in Table 5.6.[20]

The likelihood functions in the heterogeneous preferences and two-error models incorporate a constraint that requires the demand curve to be downward-sloping in the range of observed prices.[21] Therefore, we are assured of obtaining demand curves that can be used to estimate consumer surplus losses. However, if demand is downward-sloping only because the constraint is binding, one might question whether the structure of the model accurately represents consumer behavior.

Table 5.6

Maximum Likelihood Model Specifications

Model	Source(s) of Error
Heterogeneous preferences	Unobserved household characteristics
Error perception	Actual water use differs from intended water use
Two-error	Unobserved household characteristics Actual water use differs from intended water use

---

[20] Note that none of the maximum likelihood models take advantage of the panel data set as the fixed effects models do. It may be possible to combine the two approaches by allowing for a household-specific dummy variable or error term in the maximum likelihood model. However, this would require additional conceptual work to specify the likelihood function, and would be more computationally intensive than the models presented here.

[21] See Appendix D for a more detailed discussion of the nature of this constraint. In any particular case, the constraint may or may not be binding.

Estimating the maximum likelihood models was very computer intensive.[22] Because of limited computer resources, we were unable to estimate multiple specifications of the models with drought management policy variables, as was done with the OLS and fixed effects models. We will discuss the possible biases in our estimates due to omitting these variables below.

Results of the maximum likelihood estimation are shown in Table 5.7. The OLS Model 1 estimate is shown for comparison purposes. Graphs of the underlying demand curves are shown in Figures 5.7-5.9. As the figures show, both the heterogeneous preferences model and the two-error model yield downward-sloping demand curves. In the heterogeneous preferences model, the slope constraint is not binding. The change in the specification of the model by itself yields downward-sloping demand. However, the constraint is binding for the two-error model (i.e., it forces the demand curve to be downward-sloping in the observed price range). The error perception model, which is not constrained to be downward-sloping, yields results similar to the OLS and fixed effects models.

Since we now have two downward-sloping demand curves that could be used to estimate consumer surplus losses, we must consider which is a more accurate reflection of household water demand. Note that the heterogeneous preferences model yields a much less elastic demand curve than the two-error model.[23] Elasticity estimates from the two models

---

[22] Each maximum likelihood model required approximately 500 hours of offpeak computer time (over a one-month period) to converge using GAUSS software on a Sun Sparc10. The models took so long to estimate both because of the large number of observations and the complex nonlinear functions that were maximized.

[23] This occurs because the heterogeneous preferences model assumes that observed consumption is equal to intended consumption. Therefore, use in the high blocks must result from unobserved characteristics of households. Since the two-error model also allows households to make "mistakes" in consumption, the estimate of "true" demand can be more elastic, because there are two potential sources of error. In other words, the probability of a high draw from each error term in the two-error model is not as low as the probability of a very high draw from one error term in the heterogeneous preferences model.

Table 5.7

Estimated Maximum Likelihood Coefficients and t-Statistics
(Dependent Variable: Bimonthly Water Use in CCF)

Variable	OLS Model 1	Heterogeneous Preferences	Error Perception	Two-Error
Constant	-32.353	-51.453	-41.227	-40.939
(estimate/std. err.)	(-22.19)	(-40.50)	(-19.07)	(-28.33)
House size	0.0064	0.0063	0.0065	0.0064
	(28.56)	(26.97)	(26.31)	(27.04)
Lot size	0.0011	0.0012	0.0013	0.0012
	(19.62)	(20.30)	(20.41)	(20.33)
Precipitation	-0.3524	-0.6306	-0.7692	-0.7419
	(-5.14)	(-9.59)	(-10.79)	(-11.07)
Lagged precipitation	-1.0039	-1.0044	-1.1203	-1.1372
	(-16.72)	(-15.25)	(-15.59)	(-16.80)
Average temperature	0.2865	0.6797	0.6818	0.6836
	(14.94)	(47.31)	(44.56)	(46.84)
Lagged average temperature	0.6483	0.4134	0.4114	0.3967
	(34.95)	(28.82)	(27.20)	(27.23)
Price	-19.244	-4.0131	-19.014	-15.204
	(-13.81)	(-6.42)	(-8.91)	(-17.67)
Price^2	6.7308	0.2012	5.4117	2.3555
	(18.34)	(2.29)	(9.22)	(17.67)
Variance	209.26			
	(135.18)			
Variance (het. pref.)		224.81		121.69
		(134.82)		(27.96)
Variance (error per.)			227.76	104.40
			(131.73)	(25.01)
Mean log likelihood	-4.0907	-4.0863	-3.9724	-4.0791

NOTE: Constraint that demand is downward-sloping is binding in the two-error model, but not in the heterogeneous preferences model.

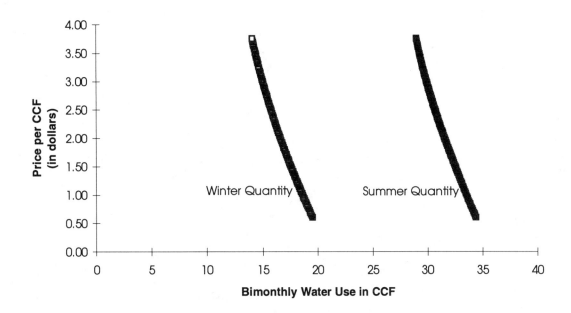

**Figure 5.7--Winter and Summer Demand Curves Based on
Heterogeneous Preferences Model**

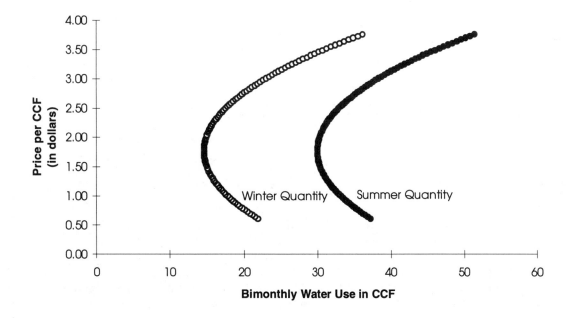

**Figure 5.8--Winter and Summer Demand Curves Based on
Error Perception Model**

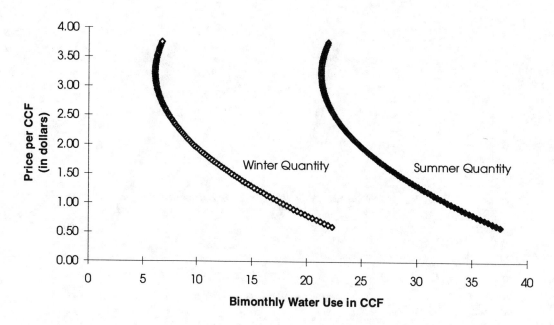

Figure 5.9--Winter and Summer Demand Curves Based on Two-Error Model

(evaluated at median house size and lot size and average summer and winter precipitation and temperatures) are shown in Table 5.8. They range from -0.04 (at a price of $0.60 per CCF) to -0.14 (at a price of $3.75 per CCF) in the summer and from -0.07 (at a price of $0.60 per CCF) to -0.29 (at a price of $3.75 per CCF) in the winter in the heterogeneous preferences model, compared with -0.20 (at a price of $0.60 per CCF) to -0.47 (at a price of $2.00 per CCF) in the summer and -0.33 (at a price of $0.60 per CCF) to -1.24 (at a price of $2.20 per CCF) in the winter in the two-error model.[24] Thus, the heterogeneous preferences model predicts relatively small cutbacks in response to price increases, whereas the two-error model predicts larger cutbacks.

---

[24]Arc elasticities from a price of $0.60 to a price of $3.75 for the heterogeneous preferences model are -0.12 in the summer and -0.22 in the winter. Arc elasticities for the two-error model are -0.38 in the summer (from $0.60 to $2.00) and -0.78 in the winter (from $0.60 to $2.20). Demand elasticity begins to decline at higher price levels in the two-error model because the curvature of demand increases.

Table 5.8

Elasticity Estimates from Maximum Likelihood Models

Model	Elasticity Estimates			
	Minimum	At Price	Maximum	At Price
Heterogeneous preferences				
Summer	-0.04	$0.60	-0.14	$3.75
Winter	-0.07	0.60	-0.29	3.75
Two-error				
Summer	-0.20	0.60	-0.47	2.00
Winter	-0.33	0.60	-1.24	2.20

NOTE: Elasticity is estimated at a point on the demand curve using the formula $(\partial Q/\partial p)\cdot(p/Q)$.

Because the slope constraint is not binding in the heterogeneous preferences model, we can feel more confident about the specification of the model. However, the two-error model specification seems intuitively more plausible, since it is probably true both that the researcher cannot observe all relevant characteristics of the household and also that households cannot always fully control their water use. Another potential piece of evidence involves the predicted effects of the two models on total water use and total water agency revenues from single-dwelling units. These predictions can be compared with aggregate data collected from Alameda County Water District as part of the survey discussed in Sections 3 and 4.

Predicting water use by households with the maximum likelihood models depends on the household's demand at each of the block rate prices. For example, during the period from July to December 1991, if the household's predicted demand at $0.90 per CCF is less than 28 CCF, that would be its predicted water use. If the household's predicted demand at $0.90 per CCF is greater than 28 CCF, its demand must be recomputed at $1.80 per CCF. Three outcomes are possible. First, if predicted demand at $1.80 per CCF is less than 28 CCF, the household's predicted water use is 28 CCF. Second, if predicted demand is between 28 and 38 CCF, that is the household's predicted use. Third, if predicted demand is above 38 CCF, demand must be computed at the next higher block rate. This process continues until the household's predicted water use is determined. The process is summarized in Table 5.9. Similar calculations can be made for January-June 1992, and July-

Table 5.9

Predicting Water Use Using Maximum Likelihood Models

If ...	Then ...
Predicted use at $0.90 ≤ 28 CCF	Predicted use = predicted use at $0.90
Predicted use at $0.90 > 28 CCF	Estimate use at $1.80
Predicted use at $1.80 ≤ 28 CCF	Predicted use = 28 CCF
28 CCF ≤ predicted use at $1.80 ≤ 38 CCF	Predicted use = predicted use at $1.80
Predicted use at $1.80 > 38 CCF	Estimate use at $2.70
Predicted use at $2.70 ≤ 38 CCF	Predicted use = 38 CCF
38 CCF ≤ predicted use at $2.70 ≤ 48 CCF	Predicted use = predicted use at $2.70
Predicted use at $2.70 > 48 CCF	Estimate use at $3.60
Predicted use at $3.60 ≤ 48 CCF	Predicted use = 48 CCF
Predicted use at $3.60 > 48 CCF	Predicted use = predicted use at $3.60

NOTE: Predicted use at higher block rates only needs to be calculated if predicted use at lower rates exceeds the maximum block water use at that price.

December 1992, using the block rate price structures and block sizes that were in effect during those periods.

Table 5.10 shows total use and revenues for households in single-dwelling units from the ACWD survey response and predicted values that are derived from the maximum likelihood models during several time periods.[25] The heterogeneous preferences model prediction is very close to actual water use by households in single-dwelling units, whereas the two-error model underpredicts by about 10 percent. Both models tend to underpredict revenue, which probably reflects underprediction of water use in the highest blocks. However, it appears that the less elastic, heterogeneous preferences (het. pref.) model is better than the two-error model as a predictor of both water use and revenues.

---

[25] ACWD's total residential accounts as of 1991 were 63,069 single-dwelling units, and 2,251 multiple-dwelling units, so approximately 97 percent were single-dwelling unit accounts. However, we expect multiple-dwelling unit accounts to have higher water use and revenue, so we adjusted the proportion to 90 percent.

Table 5.10

Actual Versus Predicted Water Use and Revenues

Single-Dwelling Unit:	Time Period	Actual	Het. Pref. Model Predicted	Two-Error Model Predicted
Water use in CCF	7/91-9/91	3,057,640	3,171,553	2,799,475
	10/91-12/91	2,481,357	2,254,802	2,145,462
	7/91-12/91	5,538,997	5,426,355	4,944,937
Revenue	7/91-6/92	$12,855,600	$11,557,711	$9,997,248

NOTE: Time periods are chosen to correspond with ACWD's survey responses regarding quarterly water use and fiscal year revenues. Actual water use and revenues are adjusted downward by 10 percent to account for the inclusion of use and revenues for multiple-dwelling units in the total residential figures reported by ACWD. Predicted water use is adjusted upward by approximately 16 percent to account for the discrepancy between 63,069 reported single-dwelling unit accounts and 54,488 single-dwelling units in the tax assessor data.

CONSUMER SURPLUS LOSSES

Our next step is to use the heterogeneous preferences model and the two-error model to estimate total consumer surplus losses incurred by households living in single-dwelling units in ACWD, based on the 54,488 households in the tax assessor data.[26] We measured cutbacks in household water use under the block rate price structure relative to predicted demand if the lowest block rate price had been charged for all water use. Figures 5.10 and 5.11 superimpose the increasing block rate structure that was in effect from July 1, 1991, to December 31, 1991, on

---

[26] Since we were unable to include drought management policy variables because of the large amounts of computational time required, the two models measure only consumer surplus losses due to price increases during the drought. Type-of-use restrictions may have caused additional losses if consumers would have been willing to pay the higher block rates for prohibited uses.

Another caveat is that we are considering demand for water in isolation from other goods. In practice, if the price of water goes up, there are both substitution and income effects, and the household also adjusts its consumption of other goods. We are unable to estimate the income elasticity of water demand because our measure of income (from census data) is imprecise and collinear with the house size and lot size variables. Therefore, this analysis assumes that income elasticity is zero and does not control for income effects. This is likely to result in a slight overestimate of consumer surplus losses, assuming income elasticity is positive.

the demand curves generated by the two models. As shown in Figure 5.10, the heterogeneous preferences model predicts that a household of median house size and lot size would choose water use in the second block ($1.80 per CCF) during the summer, resulting in a transfer of revenues to ACWD and a relatively small deadweight loss (or loss in the value of water use to the household). The two-error model shown in Figure 5.11 predicts that the same household would cut its water use back to 28 CCF during the summer to remain in the lowest block. Thus, there would be no transfer of revenue to ACWD, but the household would experience a relatively larger deadweight loss.

Bimonthly consumer surplus losses for each household in the tax assessor data were predicted using the price structures in effect during July-December 1991, January-June 1992, and July-December 1992, weather data over the same period, and tax assessor data on the house size and lot size of each single-dwelling unit.[27] As illustrated in Figures

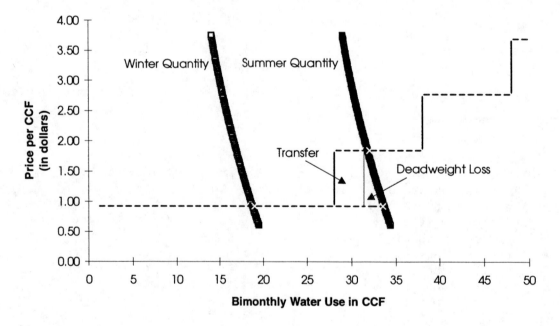

Figure 5.10--Consumer Surplus Loss, Heterogeneous Preferences Model

_____

[27] Because census variables were not used in the maximum likelihood models, the households that could not be matched to census tracts did not need to be dropped.

5.10-5.11, total consumer surplus losses are broken down into transfers of revenue to ACWD (based on higher prices paid for water consumed) and deadweight losses (based on reductions in water use). Table 5.11 shows predicted average consumer surplus losses per household and Table 5.12 shows predicted total consumer surplus losses for households living in single-dwelling units in ACWD, for each of the two models. All values are adjusted to 1992 dollars to account for inflation during the period.

The heterogeneous preferences model, which predicts less elastic demand for water, results in higher consumer surplus losses, as shown in Tables 5.11 and 5.12. However, the deadweight loss is generally smaller than in the two-error model because the heterogeneous preferences model predicts that households are more likely to pay a higher price to maintain their water use, rather than cutting back. Thus, transfer payments to ACWD are predicted to be relatively higher.[28] In contrast, the more elastic demand predicted by the two-error model results in

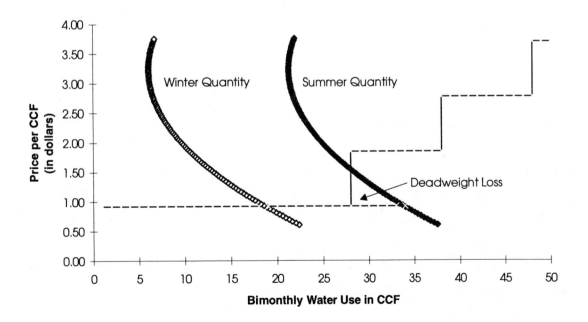

Figure 5.11--Consumer Surplus Loss, Two-Error Model

---

[28] Although transfer payments are not a net social loss, because ACWD receives them as revenue, they do represent a loss to consumers.

Table 5.11

Predicted Average Consumer Surplus Loss for Households in Single-Dwelling Units

Model	Predicted Value	July-Dec. 1991	Jan.-June 1992	July-Dec. 1992	Total
Heterogeneous preferences	Transfer to ACWD	$11.10	$5.67	$3.13	$19.90
	Deadweight loss	2.21	1.05	0.14	3.40
	Total consumer surplus loss	$13.31	$6.72	$3.27	$23.30
Two-Error	Transfer to ACWD	$ 3.20	$1.71	$1.98	$ 6.89
	Deadweight loss	4.45	1.88	.55	6.88
	Total consumer surplus loss	$ 7.65	$3.59	$2.53	$13.77

NOTE: Since consumer surplus is a nonlinear function of the coefficient estimates and independent variables, calculation of confidence limits for consumer surplus would require bootstrapping. This is likely to be very computationally intensive because of the complexity of the models and the large number of observations and was beyond the scope of this study.

lower overall consumer surplus losses. Because predicted cutbacks are larger, relatively more of the loss is a deadweight loss, and relatively less is a transfer to ACWD.

Consumer surplus losses predicted by both models are influenced by the weather and by changes in the block rate price structure. During the hottest, driest months (particularly July-October 1991), consumer surplus losses are the greatest. The losses decrease in 1992 because of cooler, wetter weather in the first half of the year, and because of a change in the block rate structure in the second half of the year. As of July 1, 1992, block sizes were increased, and the rate of price increase across blocks became less steep. The models predict that this causes households to cut back less on their water use, so deadweight losses fall and transfers to ACWD rise as a proportion of total consumer surplus losses.

Table 5.12

**Predicted Total Consumer Surplus Losses for Households
in Single-Dwelling Units**

Model	Predicted Value	July-Dec. 1991	Jan.-June 1992	July-Dec. 1992	Total
Heterogeneous preferences	Transfer to ACWD	$604,603	$309,110	$170,660	$1,084,373
	Deadweight loss	120,300	57,074	7,847	185,221
	Total consumer surplus loss	$724,903	$366,184	$178,507	$1,269,594
Two-error	Transfer to ACWD	$174,267	$ 92,862	$107,797	$ 374,926
	Deadweight loss	242,245	103,010	30,095	375,350
	Total consumer surplus loss	$416,512	$195,872	$137,892	$ 750,276

NOTE: These predictions are based on the 54,488 households in the tax assessor data. These estimates could be scaled up by approximately 16 percent to reflect ACWD's 63,069 single-dwelling unit accounts if one assumes that the distribution of house size and lot size for the additional households is the same as for the tax assessor data.

As discussed above, it appears that the heterogeneous preferences model is a better predictor of total water use and revenues for households in single-dwelling units in ACWD than the two-error model. Thus, we might also consider it a better predictor of the consumer surplus losses due to price increases than the two-error model. The heterogeneous preference model predicts larger consumer surplus losses than the two-error model, but excluding the drought management variables from these models may cause both of them to understate the consumer surplus losses due to price increases. This could occur because price increases are highly correlated with the imposition of other drought management policies, and omitting the drought policy variables may cause us to overestimate the sensitivity of water use to price. This effect can be seen in the OLS and fixed-effects models. Because consumer surplus losses are lower the more sensitive water use is to price, excluding drought policy variables may cause the estimate of consumer surplus losses to be too low.

How do these estimates of consumer surplus losses relate to the willingness-to-pay by households in single-dwelling units to avoid the ACWD's combined drought management strategies? On the one hand, these estimates may understate the willingness-to-pay to avoid the drought because they do not include welfare losses from type-of-use restrictions. Our evaluation of type-of-use restrictions in Section 4, however, concluded that type-of-use restrictions may not have been a great source of welfare loss during the drought, so this factor may not be very significant. On the other hand, these consumer surplus estimates may overstate the willingness-to-pay because they do not explicitly consider any inward shifts in the demand curve due to public education or device distribution. Such shifts would reduce the willingness-to-pay to avoid drought management strategies.

How these opposing biases balance out in this case is unknown and is complicated by the fact that we do not know how accurately the estimated demand curves are capturing the relationship between water use and price when all other policies are fixed. Further modeling and statistical estimation of water demand is needed to build confidence in our understanding of customer responses to drought management policies and the methodology of deriving willingness-to-pay from demand relationships.

These results should not be simply extrapolated to other water districts or to other parts of the state. First, water demand relationships could vary in ways that are not captured by the models estimated here. Second, as shown in Section 4, water districts across the state adopted different drought management policies, with possibly very different effects on willingness-to-pay.

6. CONCLUSION

The 1986-1992 drought caused most urban water agencies to adopt policies to reduce water consumption in their service areas. These policies determined how much customers reduced water use. Understanding the distribution of monetary and nonmonetary losses among customer classes caused by these reductions is important because this knowledge should enter into decisions on how to allocate water among competing uses and whether or not to invest in new water projects.

The maximum amount that water users would have been willing to pay to avoid drought management policies is a useful measure of the losses caused by the drought. The drought potentially generates willingness-to-pay to avoid the need for drought policies by affecting residential use, government use, and the wages, salaries, and profits generated by businesses.

For the most part, this study does not attempt to quantify the willingness-to-pay; rather, it reports the results of a survey of urban water agencies to provide the background information needed for future studies that do attempt this quantification. The survey data presented in this report suggest when and where the drought effects were most severe and how the effects were distributed across customer classes. As an illustration of the use of willingness-to-pay to avoid cutbacks in water use, this report includes a pilot study of residential consumer surplus losses due to the drought, based on water use in Alameda County Water District.

STUDY FINDINGS

Data provided by the 85 urban water agencies responding to the survey suggested that drought effects were felt primarily in 1991. Effects may well have persisted into 1992, but we were only able to collect data through 1991. Evidence suggests, however, that drought effects in urban areas subsided somewhat in 1992.

It appears that the effects of the drought on water consumption were widespread in 1991. A significant number of customers violated

quantity restrictions and paid a sizable amount in fines and rate
surcharges. Our findings suggest that effects were focused in the
residential sector, which made nearly a 20 percent cutback in 1991 water
use per-capita relative to 1986. Given that residential use accounts
for approximately two-thirds of overall urban water use, this suggests
that studies to quantify aggregate drought effects should focus on the
residential sector. Our pilot study of residential welfare losses due
to the drought found average losses per household in the range of $14 to
$23 over the period from July 1991 to December 1992. However, this
study only included losses due to price increases. We were not able to
model the effects of other drought management policies. This may have
caused us to overestimate welfare losses if other drought management
policies (such as public education or device distribution) shifted the
demand curve, or to underestimate welfare losses if type-of-use
restrictions prohibited high-value uses.

Water use also declined substantially in the commercial and
industrial sectors (15 percent and 20 percent, respectively, between
1986 and 1991). This is somewhat surprising, because the survey
responses suggest that these sectors were shielded to a large extent
from drought management policies, but the large declines were probably
due in part to factors other than the drought. The economic recession
that affected California in 1990-1991 most likely had an important
effect on water use and economic activity. The drought was probably the
overriding factor explaining reduction in residential water use, but the
importance of the drought relative to other factors is less clear for
the commercial and industrial sectors. The shielding of commercial and
industrial users from drought management policies suggests that wages,
salaries, and profits on the whole were not substantially affected by
the drought, although there were likely certain subsectors of the
economy, such as the landscaping industry, where the effects were
significant.[1] The large declines in water use relative to wages and
salaries also suggests that the commercial and industrial sectors were
able to make at least some reductions in water use without substantial

_____

[1]Note that depressed activity during the drought may possibly be
compensated for by greater activity than normal after the drought.

cuts in wages, salaries, and profits, but further evidence is needed to confirm this hypothesis.

NEXT STEPS

It proved very difficult to collect the information needed to characterize urban drought effects. A lengthy survey instrument was required and the response rate was low. Many agencies were able to fill out only some parts of the survey. Our experience illustrates how difficult, and expensive, it currently is to do detailed analyses of drought situations and probably explains why such analyses have not been done more frequently in the past. Urban water agencies may want to consider improving their data collection and reporting programs to make such evaluations easier.

A more structured analysis to isolate drought effects from confounding factors (particularly the 1990-1991 recession) is necessary. One possible way to do this is to correlate differences in drought management policies with changes in economic activity across regions. For example, variations in water supply conditions across the Bay Area, the Los Angeles area, and Sacramento might be used to isolate drought effects. Examining changes in commercial and industrial water use, wages and salaries, and profits during past recessions would also be helpful. The data collected for this study could be the starting point for such studies, because these data provide information on drought management policies and water cutbacks by region and by customer class. However, they would need to be matched with more detailed data on local economic conditions.

The data collected for this study could also be helpful in additional studies that attempt to quantify the willingness-to-pay. If surveys were used to directly elicit the willingness-to-pay, the data collected here could be used to create realistic scenarios of likely drought consequences for the respondent to consider. Data on penalties paid and increased water costs could possibly be used to provide a lower bound on the willingness-to-pay.

Further statistical work on water use data from additional water districts is needed to identify the appropriate modeling approaches and to determine whether they are generalizable across water districts. The pilot study on residential losses due to the drought illustrates the difficulties involved in using demand curve analysis to estimate willingness-to-pay. Sophisticated statistical techniques were needed to analyze customer responses to increased block rate structures and to generate demand curves that could be used to estimate consumer surplus losses. Better knowledge of water demand would allow us to make better assessments of the effectiveness of past drought management policies, and to design better drought management policies for the future.

Finally, the survey data collected for this study could be used as the basis for a study of the effectiveness of drought management strategies by correlating information on customer responses with the mixes of drought management policies implemented by the survey respondents. An analysis of this type could determine which policies are most effective in achieving target cutbacks, although data on willingness-to-pay would also be needed to determine which policies achieve target cutbacks with a minimum of economic harm. Information on the effectiveness of various drought management policies may be of particular interest to urban water agencies as they plan for the next drought.

Appendix

A. SURVEY INSTRUMENT

A copy of the key portions of the survey instrument sent to urban water agencies follows in this appendix. To save space, we photoreduced the survey and omitted section title pages and pages containing only general directions. We also have not included pages that differ only in that they collect data for different years. We have noted where such pages are excluded. The actual survey instrument is available from the authors.

1) **For the years 1986 - 1991 what were your total Water Agency Revenues in thousands of dollars from the following revenue sources? Include drought penalties or surcharges. If revenues from each customer type are not available, please provide as detailed a breakdown as possible and indicate how the customer types are aggregated. (If you can provide a breakdown only by meter size, please call RAND and we will provide an alternative survey format.)**

Water Agency Revenues

CUSTOMER TYPE	01/01/86 - 12/31/86 (in thousands)	01/01/87 - 12/31/87 (in thousands)	01/01/88 - 12/31/88 (in thousands)	01/01/89 - 12/31/89 (in thousands)	01/01/90 - 12/31/90 (in thousands)	01/01/91 - 12/31/91 (in thousands)
Residential						
Single Dwelling Unit	$	$	$	$	$	$
Multiple Dwelling Unit	$	$	$	$	$	$
OR Total Residential	$	$	$	$	$	$
Commercial	$	$	$	$	$	$
Industrial	$	$	$	$	$	$
Public Authority/Institutional	$	$	$	$	$	$
Agriculture/Horticulture	$	$	$	$	$	$
Resale/Wholesale	$	$	$	$	$	$
Other (please specify)						
_____	$	$	$	$	$	$
_____	$	$	$	$	$	$
WATER SERVICES (e.g., ground water replenishment, fire protection, etc.)	$	$	$	$	$	$
All Other Sources of Revenue (e.g., tax, hydropower, etc.)	$	$	$	$	$	$
TOTAL OPERATING REVENUES (in thousands)	$	$	$	$	$	$

2) How many <u>retail accounts</u> did you have at the end of these calendar years for the following customer types? If numbers of accounts for each customer type are not available, indicate how the customer types are aggregated.

Number of Retail Accounts by Customer Class

CUSTOMER TYPE	December 31, 1986	December 31, 1987	December 31, 1988	December 31, 1989	December 31, 1990	December 31, 1991
Residential						
Single Dwelling Unit						
Multiple Dwelling Unit						
OR Total Residential						
Commercial						
Industrial						
Public Authority/Institutional						
Agriculture/Horticulture						
Resale/Wholesale						
Other (please specify)						
_____						
_____						
Total Retail Accounts						
Total Estimated Population in Retail Area						
Total Estimated Population in Wholesale Area, if Applicable						

If you answered this question, go to Page 8.

3) How many <u>retail accounts</u> did you have at the end of these calendar years for the following meter sizes?

Number of Retail Accounts by Meter Size

METER SIZE	December 31, 1986	December 31, 1987	December 31, 1988	December 31, 1989	December 31, 1990	December 31, 1991
3/4 inch and less						
1 inch						
1 1/2 inch						
2 inch						
3 inch						
4 inch						
6 inch						
8 inch						
10 inch						
12 inch						
> 12 inch						
Total Retail Accounts						
Total Estimated Population in Retail Area						
Total Estimated Population in Wholesale Area, if Applicable						

4) For each meter size, what was the <u>percentage of accounts</u> in each customer type in 1991?

Percent of Meters in 1991						
	Residential		Commercial	Industrial	All Other	Total
Meter Size	Single family	Multiple family				
5/8 x 3/4 in.	▢ % +	▢ % +	▢ % +	▢ % +	▢ % =	100 %
3/4 in.	▢ % +	▢ % +	▢ % +	▢ % +	▢ % =	100 %
1 in.	▢ % +	▢ % +	▢ % +	▢ % +	▢ % =	100 %
1-1/2 in.	▢ % +	▢ % +	▢ % +	▢ % +	▢ % =	100 %
2 in.	▢ % +	▢ % +	▢ % +	▢ % +	▢ % =	100 %
3 in.	▢ % +	▢ % +	▢ % +	▢ % +	▢ % =	100 %
4 in.	▢ % +	▢ % +	▢ % +	▢ % +	▢ % =	100 %
6 in.	▢ % +	▢ % +	▢ % +	▢ % +	▢ % =	100 %
8 in.	▢ % +	▢ % +	▢ % +	▢ % +	▢ % =	100 %
10 in.	▢ % +	▢ % +	▢ % +	▢ % +	▢ % =	100 %
12 in.	▢ % +	▢ % +	▢ % +	▢ % +	▢ % =	100 %

5) How much water did your agency obtain from each of your water sources in 1986 and 1991, and what were the source of supply or pumping cost per unit and treatment cost per unit (if applicable)? For agency owned sources, exclude depreciation and capital recovery costs.

Please specify units (e.g., CCF, HCF, AF, MG, Thou. Gal.): _____

Amount and Cost of Water

WATER SOURCES	January 1, 1986 - December 31, 1986			January 1, 1991 - December 31, 1991		
	Amount	Source of Supply / Pumping Cost Per Unit	Treatment Cost Per Unit (if Applicable)	Amount	Source of Supply / Pumping Cost Per Unit	Treatment Cost Per Unit (if Applicable)
Agency Owned Water						
_____	▢	$ ▢	$ ▢	▢	$ ▢	$ ▢
_____	▢	$ ▢	$ ▢	▢	$ ▢	$ ▢
_____	▢	$ ▢	$ ▢	▢	$ ▢	$ ▢
Purchased Water						
_____	▢	$ ▢	$ ▢	▢	$ ▢	$ ▢
_____	▢	$ ▢	$ ▢	▢	$ ▢	$ ▢
_____	▢	$ ▢	$ ▢	▢	$ ▢	$ ▢
Recycled Water						
_____	▢	$ ▢	$ ▢	▢	$ ▢	$ ▢
Other (please specify)						
_____	▢	$ ▢	$ ▢	▢	$ ▢	$ ▢
_____	▢	$ ▢	$ ▢	▢	$ ▢	$ ▢
TOTAL WATER SUPPLY	▢			▢		

6) For the years 1986 - 1991 what were your <u>quarterly water sales</u> for the following customer classes? (If you can provide a breakdown only by meter size, please call RAND and we will provide you with an alternative survey format.)

How frequently are meters read?: _____

Please specify units (eg. CCF, HCF, AF, MG, Thou. Gal.): _____

Quarterly Water Sales From Meter Reads 1986

CUSTOMER TYPE	01/01/86 - 03/31/86	04/01/86 - 06/30/86	07/01/86 - 09/31/86	10/01/86 - 12/31/86
Residential				
Single Dwelling Unit				
Multiple Dwelling Unit				
OR Total Residential				
Commercial				
Industrial				
Public Authority/Institutional				
Agriculture/Horticulture				
Resale/Wholesale				
Other (please specify)				
_____				
_____				
Total Water Delivered				
Unaccounted for Water (Losses)				
Water Self-Supplied by Customers (e.g., pumped ground water)				

NOTE: This page was repeated for years 1987 to 1991.

7) Please indicate what <u>public education programs</u> were implemented and how much was spent on these programs per year (including both external and staff costs).

☐ No public education programs (GO TO NEXT PAGE)

Public Education Programs

Type of Program (please check)	1986	1987	1988	1989	1990	1991
Bill insert	☐	☐	☐	☐	☐	☐
TV	☐	☐	☐	☐	☐	☐
Radio	☐	☐	☐	☐	☐	☐
Newspaper	☐	☐	☐	☐	☐	☐
School Programs	☐	☐	☐	☐	☐	☐
Public displays	☐	☐	☐	☐	☐	☐
Other (please specify) _____	☐	☐	☐	☐	☐	☐
_____	☐	☐	☐	☐	☐	☐
Amount Spent	$ ☐☐☐,☐☐☐	$ ☐☐☐,☐☐☐	$ ☐☐☐,☐☐☐	$ ☐☐☐,☐☐☐	$ ☐☐☐,☐☐☐	$ ☐☐☐,☐☐☐

8. Please indicate the <u>number of water audits</u> conducted, if applicable, and total spending in each year.

☐ No water audits (GO TO NEXT PAGE)

Number of Water Audits

Customer Class	1986	1987	1988	1989	1990	1991
Residential						
Both Indoor and Outdoor	☐,☐☐	☐,☐☐	☐,☐☐	☐,☐☐	☐,☐☐	☐,☐☐
Indoor Only	☐,☐☐	☐,☐☐	☐,☐☐	☐,☐☐	☐,☐☐	☐,☐☐
Outdoor Only	☐,☐☐	☐,☐☐	☐,☐☐	☐,☐☐	☐,☐☐	☐,☐☐
Commercial						
Both Indoor and Outdoor	☐,☐☐	☐,☐☐	☐,☐☐	☐,☐☐	☐,☐☐	☐,☐☐
Indoor Only	☐,☐☐	☐,☐☐	☐,☐☐	☐,☐☐	☐,☐☐	☐,☐☐
Outdoor Only	☐,☐☐	☐,☐☐	☐,☐☐	☐,☐☐	☐,☐☐	☐,☐☐
Industrial						
Both Indoor and Outdoor	☐,☐☐	☐,☐☐	☐,☐☐	☐,☐☐	☐,☐☐	☐,☐☐
Indoor Only	☐,☐☐	☐,☐☐	☐,☐☐	☐,☐☐	☐,☐☐	☐,☐☐
Outdoor Only	☐,☐☐	☐,☐☐	☐,☐☐	☐,☐☐	☐,☐☐	☐,☐☐
Public Authority/Institutional						
Both Indoor and Outdoor	☐,☐☐	☐,☐☐	☐,☐☐	☐,☐☐	☐,☐☐	☐,☐☐
Indoor Only	☐,☐☐	☐,☐☐	☐,☐☐	☐,☐☐	☐,☐☐	☐,☐☐
Outdoor Only	☐,☐☐	☐,☐☐	☐,☐☐	☐,☐☐	☐,☐☐	☐,☐☐
Large Turf Area	☐,☐☐	☐,☐☐	☐,☐☐	☐,☐☐	☐,☐☐	☐,☐☐
Total Amount Spent	$ ☐☐☐,☐☐☐	$ ☐☐☐,☐☐☐	$ ☐☐☐,☐☐☐	$ ☐☐☐,☐☐☐	$ ☐☐☐,☐☐☐	$ ☐☐☐,☐☐☐

9) Please indicate the <u>number of conservation kits or water saving devices</u> distributed each year, the items included in these kits, and the total amount spent on the kits and their distribution in each year, not including ULF programs.

☐ No conservation kits or water saving devices distributed (GO TO NEXT PAGE)

Number of Conservation Kits

Type of Kits by Customer Class	1986	1987	1988	1989	1990	1991
Residential	☐☐,☐☐☐	☐☐,☐☐☐	☐☐,☐☐☐	☐☐,☐☐☐	☐☐,☐☐☐	☐☐,☐☐☐
Commercial	☐☐,☐☐☐	☐☐,☐☐☐	☐☐,☐☐☐	☐☐,☐☐☐	☐☐,☐☐☐	☐☐,☐☐☐
Industrial	☐☐,☐☐☐	☐☐,☐☐☐	☐☐,☐☐☐	☐☐,☐☐☐	☐☐,☐☐☐	☐☐,☐☐☐
Other	☐☐,☐☐☐	☐☐,☐☐☐	☐☐,☐☐☐	☐☐,☐☐☐	☐☐,☐☐☐	☐☐,☐☐☐

	1986	1987	1988	1989	1990	1991
Did you have a follow-up program to determine whether customers installed the kits?	☐ Yes ☐ No	☐ Yes ☐ No	☐ Yes ☐ No	☐ Yes ☐ No	☐ Yes ☐ No	☐ Yes ☐ No
Did you offer installation services?	☐ Yes ☐ No	☐ Yes ☐ No	☐ Yes ☐ No	☐ Yes ☐ No	☐ Yes ☐ No	☐ Yes ☐ No
Total Amount Spent for Purchase, Distribution, and Installation of the Kits by Your Agency	$☐☐☐,☐☐☐	$☐☐☐,☐☐☐	$☐☐☐,☐☐☐	$☐☐☐,☐☐☐	$☐☐☐,☐☐☐	$☐☐☐,☐☐☐

10a) If you had <u>conservation incentive programs for water-saving devices</u>, please indicate the dollar amount of the incentive, the number of rebates issued to each customer type, and the total amount spent on the program by year. If you need more space please xerox additional copies.

☐ No conservation incentive programs for water saving devices (GO TO PAGE 23)

Conservation Incentive Programs

	1986	1987	1988	1989	1990	1991
ULTRA LOW FLUSH TOILETS						
Amount of Rebate or Value of Incentive Per Toilet	$☐☐☐	$☐☐☐	$☐☐☐	$☐☐☐	$☐☐☐	$☐☐☐

Number of Rebates Issued
(count one per toilet)

Customer Class	1986	1987	1988	1989	1990	1991
Residential						
Single Dwelling Unit	☐☐,☐☐☐	☐☐,☐☐☐	☐☐,☐☐☐	☐☐,☐☐☐	☐☐,☐☐☐	☐☐,☐☐☐
Multiple Dwelling Unit	☐☐,☐☐☐	☐☐,☐☐☐	☐☐,☐☐☐	☐☐,☐☐☐	☐☐,☐☐☐	☐☐,☐☐☐
OR Total Residential	☐☐,☐☐☐	☐☐,☐☐☐	☐☐,☐☐☐	☐☐,☐☐☐	☐☐,☐☐☐	☐☐,☐☐☐
Commercial	☐☐,☐☐☐	☐☐,☐☐☐	☐☐,☐☐☐	☐☐,☐☐☐	☐☐,☐☐☐	☐☐,☐☐☐
Industrial	☐☐,☐☐☐	☐☐,☐☐☐	☐☐,☐☐☐	☐☐,☐☐☐	☐☐,☐☐☐	☐☐,☐☐☐
Public Authority / Institutional	☐☐,☐☐☐	☐☐,☐☐☐	☐☐,☐☐☐	☐☐,☐☐☐	☐☐,☐☐☐	☐☐,☐☐☐
All Other	☐☐,☐☐☐	☐☐,☐☐☐	☐☐,☐☐☐	☐☐,☐☐☐	☐☐,☐☐☐	☐☐,☐☐☐
Total Amount Spent on Toilet Rebate Programs per Year	$☐☐☐,☐☐☐	$☐☐☐,☐☐☐	$☐☐☐,☐☐☐	$☐☐☐,☐☐☐	$☐☐☐,☐☐☐	$☐☐☐,☐☐☐

Conservation Incentive Programs (continued)

10b. OTHER REBATE OR INCENTIVE ITEM (please describe): _____

Amount of Rebate or Value
of Incentive $ ☐☐☐.☐☐ $ ☐☐☐.☐☐ $ ☐☐☐.☐☐ $ ☐☐☐.☐☐ $ ☐☐☐.☐☐ $ ☐☐☐.☐☐

Number of Rebates Issued

Customer Class

Residential

Customer Class						
Single Dwelling Unit	☐☐,☐☐☐	☐☐,☐☐☐	☐☐,☐☐☐	☐☐,☐☐☐	☐☐,☐☐☐	☐☐,☐☐☐
Multiple Dwelling Unit	☐☐,☐☐☐	☐☐,☐☐☐	☐☐,☐☐☐	☐☐,☐☐☐	☐☐,☐☐☐	☐☐,☐☐☐
OR Total Residential	☐☐,☐☐☐	☐☐,☐☐☐	☐☐,☐☐☐	☐☐,☐☐☐	☐☐,☐☐☐	☐☐,☐☐☐
Commercial	☐☐,☐☐☐	☐☐,☐☐☐	☐☐,☐☐☐	☐☐,☐☐☐	☐☐,☐☐☐	☐☐,☐☐☐
Industrial	☐☐,☐☐☐	☐☐,☐☐☐	☐☐,☐☐☐	☐☐,☐☐☐	☐☐,☐☐☐	☐☐,☐☐☐
Public Authority / Institutional	☐☐,☐☐☐	☐☐,☐☐☐	☐☐,☐☐☐	☐☐,☐☐☐	☐☐,☐☐☐	☐☐,☐☐☐
All Other	☐☐,☐☐☐	☐☐,☐☐☐	☐☐,☐☐☐	☐☐,☐☐☐	☐☐,☐☐☐	☐☐,☐☐☐

Total Amount Spent on
Other Rebate/Incentive
Programs Per Year $ ☐☐☐,☐☐☐ $ ☐☐☐,☐☐☐ $ ☐☐☐,☐☐☐ $ ☐☐☐,☐☐☐ $ ☐☐☐,☐☐☐ $ ☐☐☐,☐☐☐

11) If your agency implemented <u>restrictions on type of use</u> between 1986 - 1991, please indicate the type of restriction (e.g., no watering of hard surfaces), the type of customers affected, whether restrictions were voluntary or mandatory, the dates effective, and penalties for violations. Please start a new line for each change in restrictions.

☐ No restrictions on type of use (GO TO NEXT PAGE)

Restrictions On Type Of Use (Please Specify)	Type of Customers Effected					Voluntary	Mandatory	Dates Effective	Describe any Penalties or Enforcement Activities
	Residential Single DU	Multiple DU	Comm.	Ind.	Other	Please use separate line if this varied by customer class.			
_____	☐	☐	☐	☐	☐	☐	☐	☐☐/☐☐/☐☐ to ☐☐/☐☐/☐☐	_____
_____	☐	☐	☐	☐	☐	☐	☐	☐☐/☐☐/☐☐ to ☐☐/☐☐/☐☐	_____
_____	☐	☐	☐	☐	☐	☐	☐	☐☐/☐☐/☐☐ to ☐☐/☐☐/☐☐	_____
_____	☐	☐	☐	☐	☐	☐	☐	☐☐/☐☐/☐☐ to ☐☐/☐☐/☐☐	_____
_____	☐	☐	☐	☐	☐	☐	☐	☐☐/☐☐/☐☐ to ☐☐/☐☐/☐☐	_____

12) If your agency implemented <u>restrictions on quantities used</u>, please indicate the type of restriction (e.g., fixed amount per household per month, percentage cutback from specified base year), the type of customers affected, whether restrictions were voluntary or mandatory, the dates effective, and penalties for violations. Please start a new line for each change in restrictions.

☐ **No restrictions on quantities used (GO TO NEXT PAGE)**

Restrictions On Quantities Use (Please specify, including base year, if applicable)	Type of Customers Effected					Voluntary Mandatory Please use separate line if this varied by customer class.		Dates Effective	Describe any Penalties or Enforcement Activities
	Residential Single DU	Multiple DU	Comm.	Ind.	Other	Voluntary	Mandatory		
_____ _____	☐	☐	☐	☐	☐	☐	☐	☐/☐☐ ☐/☐☐ to	_____ _____ _____
_____ _____	☐	☐	☐	☐	☐	☐	☐	☐/☐☐ ☐/☐☐ to	_____ _____ _____
_____ _____	☐	☐	☐	☐	☐	☐	☐	☐/☐☐ ☐/☐☐ to	_____ _____ _____
_____ _____	☐	☐	☐	☐	☐	☐	☐	☐/☐☐ ☐/☐☐ to	_____ _____ _____
_____ _____	☐	☐	☐	☐	☐	☐	☐	☐/☐☐ ☐/☐☐ to	_____ _____ _____

13a) If your agency had <u>surcharges or penalty rates for exceeding base quantity allocations</u> assessed as part of the customer's water bill, please indicate the number of customers penalized and total penalties billed by customer type.

☐ **No surcharge or penalty rates for exceeding base quantity allocations (GO TO NEXT PAGE)**

Number of Customers Assessed Surcharges

Customer Type	1986	1987	1988	1989	1990	1991
Residential						
Single Dwelling Unit						
Multiple Dwelling Unit						
OR Total Residential						
Commercial						
Industrial						
Public Authority/ Institutional						
All Other						

Surcharges Billed (in Thousands)

Customer Type	1986	1987	1988	1989	1990	1991
Residential						
Single Dwelling Unit	$	$	$	$	$	$
Multiple Dwelling Unit	$	$	$	$	$	$
OR Total Residential	$	$	$	$	$	$
Commercial	$	$	$	$	$	$
Industrial	$	$	$	$	$	$
Public Authority/Institutional	$	$	$	$	$	$
All Other	$	$	$	$	$	$
Total Surcharges Billed (In thousands)	$	$	$	$	$	$

13b) If your agency issued citations or otherwise <u>enforced penalties for use restrictions</u> (such as watering of hard surfaces), please indicate the number of customers penalized, total penalties billed by customer type, and the total yearly enforcement costs.

☐ No enforced penalties for use restrictions (GO TO NEXT PAGE)

Number of Customers Assessed Penalties

Customer Type	1986	1987	1988	1989	1990	1991
Residential						
Single Dwelling Unit						
Multiple Dwelling Unit						
OR Total Residential						
Commercial						
Industrial						
Public Authority/ Institutional						
All Other						

Penalties Billed (in Thousands)

Customer Type	1986	1987	1988	1989	1990	1991
Residential						
Single Dwelling Unit	$	$	$	$	$	$
Multiple Dwelling Unit	$	$	$	$	$	$
OR Total Residential	$	$	$	$	$	$
Commercial	$	$	$	$	$	$
Industrial	$	$	$	$	$	$
Public Authority/Institutional	$	$	$	$	$	$
All Other	$	$	$	$	$	$
Total Penalties Billed (In thousands)	$	$	$	$	$	$
Cost of Enforcement (in thousands)	$	$	$	$	$	$

14a) If your agency granted exemptions or appeals for water quantity or use restrictions between 1986 and 1991, please indicate the number of <u>exemptions/appeals requested (R) and granted (G)</u> for each customer type.

☐ No exemptions/appeals requested or granted (GO TO 14c)

Exemptions / Appeals Requested (R) and Granted (G)

CUSTOMER TYPE	1986 R	1986 G	1987 R	1987 G	1988 R	1988 G	1989 R	1989 G	1990 R	1990 G	1991 R	1991 G
Residential												
Single Dwelling Unit												
Multiple Dwelling Unit												
OR Total Residential												
Commercial												
Industrial												
Public Authority/Institutional												
Other (please specify)												
_____												
_____												

14b) What were the most common reasons for granting exemptions or appeals?

_____

_____

_____

_____

14c) What methods of appeal were available to customers?

_____

_____

_____

_____

15a) For the period 1986-1991, please indicate your <u>requested percentage cutbacks</u> in water use including the base year, effective dates, and every change in requested cutbacks thereafter.

Requested Water Use Cutbacks

	Dates in Effect	Dates in Effect	Dates in Effect	Dates in Effect	Dates in Effect
	□□/□□/□□ to □□/□□/□□	□□/□□/□□ to □□/□□/□□	□□/□□/□□ to □□/□□/□□	□□/□□/□□ to □□/□□/□□	□□/□□/□□ to □□/□□/□□
Base Year	19□	19□	19□	19□	19□
Overall Reduction Goal	□ %	□ %	□ %	□ %	□ %

15b) If the base year was adjusted for growth and/or climate, please indicate how this was calculated.

_____

_____

15c) If reduction goals varied by customer type, please indicate the goals for each of the following customer types:

□ Reduction goals did not vary by customer type (GO TO NEXT PAGE)

CUSTOMER TYPE

Residential

Single Dwelling Unit	□ %	□ %	□ %	□ %	□ %
Multiple Dwelling Unit	□ %	□ %	□ %	□ %	□ %
OR Total Residential	□ %	□ %	□ %	□ %	□ %
Commercial	□ %	□ %	□ %	□ %	□ %
Industrial	□ %	□ %	□ %	□ %	□ %
Public Authority/Institutional	□ %	□ %	□ %	□ %	□ %
Resale/Wholesale	□ %	□ %	□ %	□ %	□ %
Other (please specify)					
_____	□ %	□ %	□ %	□ %	□ %

16) Please list your <u>monthly service charge</u> for the following meter sizes on January 1, 1986 and for every change in rates thereafter. If monthly service charge varies by customer class, please provide rate schedules.

Monthly Service Charge

METER SIZE	1/01/86	Date of Change □□/□□/□□	Date of Change □□/□□/□□	Date of Change □□/□□/□□	Date of Change □□/□□/□□	Date of Change □□/□□/□□
5/8 x 3/4 in.	$□□□.□□	$□□□.□□	$□□□.□□	$□□□.□□	$□□□.□□	$□□□.□□
3/4 in.	$□□□.□□	$□□□.□□	$□□□.□□	$□□□.□□	$□□□.□□	$□□□.□□
1 in.	$□□□.□□	$□□□.□□	$□□□.□□	$□□□.□□	$□□□.□□	$□□□.□□
1-1/2 in.	$□□□.□□	$□□□.□□	$□□□.□□	$□□□.□□	$□□□.□□	$□□□.□□
2 in.	$□□□.□□	$□□□.□□	$□□□.□□	$□□□.□□	$□□□.□□	$□□□.□□
3 in.	$□□□.□□	$□□□.□□	$□□□.□□	$□□□.□□	$□□□.□□	$□□□.□□
4 in.	$□□□.□□	$□□□.□□	$□□□.□□	$□□□.□□	$□□□.□□	$□□□.□□
6 in.	$□□□.□□	$□□□.□□	$□□□.□□	$□□□.□□	$□□□.□□	$□□□.□□
8 in.	$□□□.□□	$□□□.□□	$□□□.□□	$□□□.□□	$□□□.□□	$□□□.□□
10 in.	$□□□.□□	$□□□.□□	$□□□.□□	$□□□.□□	$□□□.□□	$□□□.□□
12 in.	$□□□.□□	$□□□.□□	$□□□.□□	$□□□.□□	$□□□.□□	$□□□.□□

17) **If your monthly service charge includes a quantity allowance, please list your <u>monthly quantity allowance</u> on January 1, 1986 and for every change in allowance thereafter. If monthly quantity allowance differs by customer class, please provide rate schedules.**

Please specify units (e.g., CCF, HCF, AF, MG, Thou. Gal.): _____

☐ Not Applicable (GO TO NEXT PAGE)

Monthly Quantity Allowance

METER SIZE	01/01/86	Date of Change	Date of Change	Date of Change	Date of Change	Date of Change
5/8 x 3/4 in.						
3/4 in.						
1 in.						
1-1/2 in.						
2 in.						
3 in.						
4 in.						
6 in.						
8 in.						
10 in.						
12 in.						

18) **Please indicate your <u>water rates by customer type</u> on January 1, 1986 and for every rate change thereafter. If the sizes of the blocks change or you have summer and winter rates, please begin a new section if necessary. Please xerox additional sheets if your rates changed more than once a year.**

Please specify units (e.g., CCF, HCF, AF, MG, Thou. Gal.): _____

Water Rates By Customer Type

Customer Type (please specify) _____	As of 01/01/86	Date of Change	Date of Change	Date of Change	Date of Change	Date of Change

Dollars Per Unit

Block 1 (e.g., 0-500 cu. ft.) Specify: _____	$	$	$	$	$	$
Block 2 Specify: _____	$	$	$	$	$	$
Block 3 Specify: _____	$	$	$	$	$	$
Block 4 Specify: _____	$	$	$	$	$	$

Customer Type (please specify) _____	As of 01/01/86	Date of Change	Date of Change	Date of Change	Date of Change	Date of Change

Dollars Per Unit

Block 1 (e.g., 0-500 cu. ft.) Specify: _____	$	$	$	$	$	$
Block 2 Specify: _____	$	$	$	$	$	$
Block 3 Specify: _____	$	$	$	$	$	$
Block 4 Specify: _____	$	$	$	$	$	$

19a) Do you know of any urban drought impact studies about your service area?

☐ Don't Know (GO TO 19b)

<u>Group</u>	<u>Study</u>
_____	_____
_____	_____
_____	_____
_____	_____
	_____

19b) Please describe any serious concerns expressed by residential, commercial, or industrial users over water supply availability and/or quality during the drought.

☐ Don't Know (GO TO NEXT PAGE)

<u>Group</u>	<u>Concern</u>
_____	_____
_____	_____
_____	_____
_____	_____
	_____

20a) If the Drought Water Bank had not been created in 1991, we estimate that your surface water supplies would have been cut by:

☐☐☐

What <u>alternative sources</u> of supply could have been used?

☐ No alternative supplies (GO TO 20b AND ENTER "0" FOR TOTAL ALTERNATIVE WATER SUPPLIES)

Source	Alternative Water Supplies (Acre-feet)	Cost / Acre-foot *
_____	☐☐,☐☐☐	$☐,☐☐☐
_____	☐☐,☐☐☐	$☐,☐☐☐
_____	☐☐,☐☐☐	$☐,☐☐☐
_____	☐☐,☐☐☐	$☐,☐☐☐
_____	☐☐,☐☐☐	$☐,☐☐☐
_____	☐☐,☐☐☐	$☐,☐☐☐
_____	☐☐,☐☐☐	$☐,☐☐☐

⇩ ⇩

⇩ ⇩

20b) ☐☐☐☐ − ☐☐☐,☐☐☐ = ☐☐☐,☐☐☐

Water Bank Water Provided — *Total Alternative Water Supplies* — *Additional Cutbacks Needed*

* Please use same definition of cost as in Question 4.

20c) How would the <u>additional cutbacks</u> have been distributed by customer type?

☐ Cutbacks would have been spread proportionally among users (GO TO 20d)

Customer type	Water Cutback (Acre Feet)
Residential	
Single Dwelling Unit	☐☐,☐☐☐
Multiple Dwelling Unit	☐☐,☐☐☐
OR Total Residential	☐☐,☐☐☐
Commercial	☐☐,☐☐☐
Industrial	☐☐,☐☐☐
Public Authority / Institutional	☐☐,☐☐☐
Agriculture / Horticulture	☐☐,☐☐☐
Resale/Wholesale	☐☐,☐☐☐
Other (please specify)	
_____	☐☐☐,☐☐☐
_____	☐☐☐,☐☐☐
TOTAL CUTBACKS	☐☐☐,☐☐☐

NOTE: AMOUNTS SHOULD BE EQUAL

20d) If you had not received [_____] from the Drought Water Bank water in 1991, how would your drought management stages/policies have changed (e.g. what additional phases of your drought management plan would have gone into effect)?

		Please check customer type(s) the policy would have applied to:			
Stages/Policies	Changes	Residential	Commercial	Industrial	Other
Public Education		☐	☐	☐	☐
Water Audits		☐	☐	☐	☐
Device Distribution		☐	☐	☐	☐
Conservation Rebates		☐	☐	☐	☐
Use Restrictions		☐	☐	☐	☐
Quantity Restrictions		☐	☐	☐	☐
Price Increases		☐	☐	☐	☐
Other (please specify)		☐ ☐	☐ ☐	☐ ☐	☐ ☐

B. SURVEY RESPONDENTS

The 85 urban retail water agencies that responded to the survey are listed below. They are grouped by location.

San Francisco Bay Area

Marin Municipal Water District
Great Oaks Water Company
San Jose Water Co.
City of Hayward
City of Daly City
City of Milpitas
North Coast County Water
   District
Contra Costa Water District
Alameda County Water District

East Bay Municipal Utility
   District
City of San Francisco
California Water Service
 - Bear Gulch
 - San Mateo
 - Livermore
 - San Carlos
 - Los Altos
City of Santa Clara

Southern California

City of Westminster
El Toro Water District
Yorba Linda Water District
City of Garden Grove
Mesa Consolidated Water District
City of Huntington Beach
City of Buena Park
City of Long Beach
City of Manhattan Beach
Montebello Land and Water Co.
City of Corona
City of Redlands
City of Port Hueneme
City of Inglewood
Las Virgenes Municipal Water
   District
Quartz Hill Water District
City of Riverside
Jurupa Community Service
   District
Hesperia Water District
City of Glendale
Palmdale Water District
City of West Covina
Desert Water Agency
Hi-Desert Water District
City of Pico Rivera
City of Torrance

Park Water Company
City of Anaheim
City of Newport Beach
Ventura County WW #8
Padre Dam Municipal Water District
Santa Fe Irrigation District
Sweetwater Authority
City of Poway
Olivenhain Municipal Water
   District
San Dieguito Water District
Los Angeles Department of
   Water and Power
City of San Diego
California Water Service
   -Westlake District
   -East Los Angeles
   -Palos Verdes
   -Hermosa Redondo
California American
   -Baldwin Hills
   -Coronado
   -Village
City of Burbank
Lincoln Av. Water Co.
Laguna Beach Water Co.
Vallecitos Water District

Rest of the State

City of Bakersfield
Tahoe City Public Utility
  District
Citrus Heights Irrigation
  District
Northridge Water District
City of Santa Barbara
Goleta Water District
City of Tulare
San Juan Suburban Water
  District
City of Merced

Elk Grove Water District
City of Manteca
City of Fresno
City of Santa Cruz
City of Fairfield
California Water Service
  -Bakersfield
  -Salinas
  -Stockton
  -Visalia District
California American-Monterey

C. DISTRIBUTION OF 1991 DROUGHT WATER BANK PURCHASES

Estimates of the water received from the 1991 Drought Water Bank by individual water agencies are listed below. The figures listed for the 12 direct purchasers (numbered 1 through 12 below) were obtained from the California Department of Water Resources ([1992], p. 6). Of these 12 agencies, 5 (City of San Francisco, Alameda County Flood Control & Water Conservation District, Santa Clara Valley Water District, Kern County Water Agency, and the Metropolitan Water District of Southern California) passed on some share of water-bank purchases through wholesale deliveries to other agencies. Usually, the resale of water-bank supplies was not recorded separately from other wholesale deliveries, although there were a few exceptions in which agencies or individual customers requested water-bank supplies through the wholesale agencies. Therefore, we distributed water-bank deliveries among the second tier of agencies in proportion to total wholesale water deliveries (i.e., from all sources of water) to those agencies in 1991 by the original purchaser of water-bank water.

We obtained figures on 1991 wholesale water deliveries by contacting each of the five agencies. In the case of the Metropolitan Water District of Southern California (MWDSC), we contacted an additional layer of 12 wholesale water districts operating as middlemen between MWDSC and retail water agencies. In some cases, we were unable to obtain the complete names of the retail water agencies who received water-bank supplies (these names are indicated by a question mark); in the case of the City of San Francisco, we obtained delivery figures for the set of agencies in the survey sample and estimated deliveries to the remainder of San Francisco's wholesale customers.

1991 Drought Water Bank--Buyers

Water Agency	Acre-Feet
1. American Canyon County Water District	370
2. City of San Francisco (50,000 acre-feet total)	
Own retail customers	16,698
Alameda County Water District	2,150
Belmont County Water District[a]	794
City of Brisbane[a]	127
Guadeloupe Valley Municipal Improvement District[a]	23
City of Burlingame	903
California Water Service Company--Bear Gulch	2,063
California Water Service Company--San Carlos	801
California Water Service Company--San Mateo	2,492
California Water Service Company--South San Francisco[a]	1,556
Coastside County Water District[a]	451
East Palo Alto Water District[a]	408
City of Daly City	644
Estero Municipal Improvement District (Foster City)[a]	823
City of Hayward	3,463
Town of Hillsborough	614
Los Trancos County Water District (Portola Valley)[a]	26
City of Menlo Park[a]	410
City of Millbrae[a]	672
City of Milpitas	1,936
City of Mountain View	2,133
North Coast County Water District	658
City of Palo Alto	2,595
Purissima Hills Water District (Los Altos Hills)	307
City of Redwood City	2,084
City of San Bruno	413
City of Santa Clara[a]	2,488
Skyline County Water District (Woodside)[a]	47
Stanford University[a]	64
City of Sunnyvale	1,798
Westborough Water District (South San Francisco)[a]	359
3. Contra Costa Water District	6,717
4. Alameda County Water District	14,800
5. Alameda County Flood Control & Water Conservation District (500 acre-feet total)	
California Water Service Company--Livermore	137
City of Livermore	65
City of Pleasanton	234
Dublin—San Ramon Service District	64

---

[a]Estimated share of Drought Water Bank supplies based on relative number of service connections (covers 16 percent of total). Other figures were compiled by the San Francisco Water Department based on shares of water deliveries.

6. Santa Clara Valley Water District   (19,500 acre-feet total)
        California Water Service Company--Los Altos   1,175
        City of Cupertino   270
        Great Oaks Water Company   1,060
        City of Mountain View   284
        City of San Jose   1,055
        San Jose Water Company   12,063
        City of Santa Clara   1,973
        City of Sunnyvale   1,620

7. Oak Flat Water District   975

8. Westlands Water District   13,820

9. Dudley Ridge Water District   13,805

10. Kern County Water Agency   (53,997 acre-feet total)
        Berrenda Mesa Water District   47,000
        Lost Hills Water District   5,997
        Belridge Water Service District   1,000

11. Crestline--Lake Arrowhead Water Agency   236

12. Metropolitan Water District of Southern California
        (215,000 acre-feet total)
        City of Anaheim   2,597
        City of Beverly Hills   1,304
        City of Burbank   1,957
        City of Compton   417
        City of Fullerton   758
        City of Glendale   2,470
        Las Virgenes Municipal Water District   1,937
        City of Long Beach   3,802
        City of Los Angeles   30,703
        City of Pasadena   1,965
        City of San Fernando   70
        City of San Marino   78
        City of Santa Ana   2,002
        City of Santa Monica   552
        City of Torrance   1,750

        Calleguas Municipal Water District   (2,014 acre-feet from MWDSC)
            Brandeis (?)   1
            California American Water Company--Village   129
            City of Camarillo   29
            Camrosa Water District   800
            Caypart (?)   2
            Crestview Mutual Water Company   2
            Lakeshore (?)   2
            Metropolitan Water Company   30
            City of Oxnard   135
            Pleasant Valley Mutual Water Company   3

            _____

            NOTE: (?) denotes that we were unable to obtain complete name of
            retail agency.

Calleguas Municipal Water District   (continued)

Russell Valley Municipal Water District	76
Southern California Water Company--Simi Valley	67
City of Thousand Oaks	86
Ventura County Waterworks District #1 (Moorpark)	482
Ventura County Waterworks District #8 (Simi Valley)	162
Ventura County Waterworks District #19 (Somis)	8

Central Basin Municipal Water District
(13,322 acre-feet from MWDSC)

City of Bell Gardens	122
City of Bellflower	392
California Water Service Company – East L.A.	1,416
City of Cerritos	207
City of Commerce	57
Rancho Los Amigos	45
La Habra Heights Water District	20
City of Lakewood	43
City of Lynwood	188
Maywood Mutual Water Company #1 (Huntington Park)	19
Maywood Mutual Water Company #2 (Maywood)	68
City of Montebello	126
Orchard Dale Water Company	84
City of Paramount	168
Park Water Company	812
San Gabriel Valley Water Company	63
City of Santa Fe Springs	545
City of Signal Hill	44
Southern California Water Company – Metropolitan	1,372
Suburban Water Systems	401
City of Vernon	159
Walnut Park Mutual Water Company	42
Orange County Water District (ground water replenishment)	174
Water Replenishment District	6,755

Chino Basin Municipal Water District   (4,860 acre-feet from MWDSC)

City of Chino	238
Chino Hills (?)	851
Cucamonga County Water District	1,798
First City (?)	5
Monte Vista Water District	267
City of Ontario	710
Southern California Edison	63
City of Upland	452
Watermasters (?)	476

NOTE: (?) denotes that we were unable to obtain complete name of retail agency.

Coastal Municipal Water District   (5,808 acre-feet from MWDSC)
    Irvine Ranch Water District   30
    Laguna Beach County Water District   612
    City of Newport Beach   2,813
    South Coast Water District   542
    Tri-Cities Municipal Water District   1,811

Eastern Municipal Water District   (5,749 acre-feet from MWDSC)
    Own retail customers   5,265
    Direct request from real estate developer   78
    Edgemont Gardens Mutual Water Company   53
    March Air Force Base   154
    City of Perris   199

Foothill Municipal Water District   (942 acre-feet from MWDSC)
    La Cañada Irrigation District   225
    Las Flores Water Company   49
    Lincoln Avenue Water Company   138
    Mesa Crest Water Company   59
    Rubio Cañon Land & Water Association   57
    Valley County Water District   169
    Valley Water Company   245

Municipal Water District of Orange County
(22,421 acre-feet from MWDSC)
    City of Brea   707
    City of Buena Park   591
    Capistrano Valley Water District   515
    East Orange County Water District   700
    El Toro Water District   962
    City of Fountain Valley   286
    City of Garden Grove   496
    City of Huntington Beach   1,012
    Irvine Ranch Water District   2,747
    City of La Habra   151
    City of La Palma   28
    Los Alisos Water District   777
    Mesa Consolidated Water District   782
    Moulton Niguel Water District   2,839
    City of Orange   916
    Santa Ana Heights Water Company   180
    Santa Margarita Water District   1,657
    City of Seal Beach   23
    Southern California Water Company—Orange County   771
    Trabuco Canyon Water District   285
    City of Westminster   208
    Yorba Linda Water District   836
    Orange County Water District
        (ground water replenishment)   4,952

San Diego County Water Authority   (67,393 acre-feet from MWDSC)
    Bueno Colorado Municipal Water District   1,685
    Carlsbad Municipal Water District   2,046
    City of Del Mar   174
    City of Escondido   2,220
    Fallbrook Public Utility District   1,803
    Helix Water District   4,115

San Diego County Water Authority   (continued)
City of National City	424
City of Oceanside	3,301
Olivenhain Municipal Water District	1,506
Otay Water District	2,558
Padre Dam Municipal Water District	2,205
Camp Pendleton Military Reservation	13
City of Poway	1,526
Rainbow Municipal Water District	3,526
Ramona Municipal Water District	1,771
Rincon Del Diablo Municipal Water District	928
City of San Diego	26,061
San Dieguito Water District	733
Santa Fe Irrigation District	1,028
South Bay Irrigation District	2,387
Vallecitos Water District	1,504
Valley Center Municipal Water District	5,665
Yuima Municipal Water District	214

Three Valleys Municipal Water District
(6,502 acre-feet from MWDSC)
City of La Verne	1,625
City of Pomona	813
Rowland Water District	813
Southern California Water Company - Pomona	1,625
Walnut Valley Water District	1,626

Upper San Gabriel Valley Municipal Water District
(7,976 acre-feet from MWDSC)
Own retail customers	800
City of Alhambra	236
Azusa Valley Water Company	16
Valley County Water District	124
City of West Covina	758
Ground water replenishment	6,042

West Basin Municipal Water District   (17,169 acre-feet from MWDSC)
California American Water Company--Baldwin Hills	70
California Water Service Company--Palos Verdes	2,905
Dominguez Water Corporation	2,549
City of El Segundo	1,950
Chevron Oil Refinery (by request)	1,550
City of Hawthorne	294
City of Inglewood	736
City of Manhattan Beach	478
City of Lomita	254
Los Angeles County Waterworks District #1	23
Los Angeles County Waterworks District #22	21
Los Angeles County Waterworks Districts #29-56	785
Southern California Water Company--Metropolitan	2,802
Water Replenishment District	2,752

Western Municipal Water District   (8,482 acre-feet from MWDSC)
```
     Own retail customers                              3,985
     Bedford Heights (?)                                  97
     City of Corona                                    1,064
     Eagle Valley Mutual Water Company                   332
     Elsinore Valley Municipal Water District            674
     El Sobrante Water Company                           829
     March Air Force Base                                142
     Rancho California Water District                  1,116
     City of Riverside                                   243
```

NOTE: (?) denotes that we were unable to obtain complete name of
retail agency.

D. MAXIMUM LIKELIHOOD MODELS

The maximum likelihood models discussed in Section 5 of this report are based on Hewitt [1993] and Hewitt and Hanemann [1995], which provide more detail on the theoretical development of the models. The original models were developed to analyze a rate structure with two blocks, so they had to be generalized to fit the Alameda County Water District (ACWD) rate structures in effect over the period from 1982 to 1992. From 1982 through June 1991, a single-block rate structure was in effect, so the maximum likelihood model used during this period is equivalent to an OLS model. From June 1991 through June 1992, a four-block rate structure was in effect. As discussed in Section 5, the maximum likelihood models for this period differ depending on the assumptions made about the source of the estimating error. In this appendix, we discuss the specification of each of the maximum likelihood models in turn.[1]

HETEROGENEOUS PREFERENCES MODEL

In the heterogeneous preferences model, we assume that the household's observed water use is equal to its intended water use, but that we cannot observe all of the household's characteristics that influence its water use. Thus, when we estimate water use based on observable variables (such as house size, lot size, weather, etc.), an estimating error arises because of the effects of the unobservable variables.

Since we are assuming that observed water use is equal to intended water use, the household must have intended to consume in the observed block and is responding to the price associated with that block. Therefore, within any block, the error is equal to the difference

---

[1]Note that these models assume that each observation is independent and therefore do not take advantage of the panel nature of the data set. It may be possible to incorporate a fixed-effects or random-effects approach with household-specific dummy variables or error terms. However, this would require additional conceptual work to specify the likelihood functions and would be more computationally intensive than the models discussed here.

between observed water use and predicted water use (based on observable characteristics) at the price associated with that block. However, if observed water use is at the borderline between two blocks (i.e., at the "kink"), a range of error terms is possible. One possibility is that intended water use at the lower block price is exactly equal to the kink. The other possibility is that preferred water use at the lower block price is higher than the kink, but the household is not willing to pay the higher block price to increase its water use. Therefore, the error term could be one of a range of values based on the difference between intended use (equal to the kink) and predicted water use at either block price.

Equation D.1 shows the log likelihood function for the heterogeneous preferences model, assuming that the error term is normally distributed. The first term in Equation D.1 applies to periods when a single-block rate structure was in effect (1982 through June 1991), and the remaining terms apply to periods when a four-block rate structure was in effect (July 1991 through June 1992). The subscripts 1 through 4 in the remaining terms indicate that the price variables correspond with the block rate structure. For example, during the period July-December 1991, the price in block 1 was \$0.90, the price in block 2 was \$1.80, the price in block 3 was \$2.70, and the price in block 4 was \$3.60.

Since observed consumption is assumed to be equal to intended consumption, each observation y is assigned to one block or kink point. Note that the integral terms in Equation D.1 must be positive, which requires $X_1\beta > X_2\beta > X_3\beta > X_4\beta$, i.e., demand must be decreasing in price over the observed range of prices in the block rate structure. This constrains the estimated demand curve to be downward-sloping. However, as discussed in Section 5, this constraint was not binding for the estimated coefficients of the heterogeneous preferences model.

$$\ln L = \sum_{\substack{\text{Obs before} \\ \text{July 1991}}} -\frac{1}{2}\ln(2\pi\sigma_\varepsilon^2) - \frac{(y-X\beta)'(y-X\beta)}{2\sigma_\varepsilon^2}$$

$$+ \sum_{\substack{\text{Obs in} \\ \text{Block 1}}} -\frac{1}{2}\ln(2\pi\sigma_\varepsilon^2) - \frac{(y-X_1\beta)'(y-X_1\beta)}{2\sigma_\varepsilon^2} + \sum_{\substack{\text{Obs at} \\ \text{Kink 1}}} \ln\left[\int_{\text{Kink 1}-X_1\beta}^{\text{Kink 1}-X_2\beta} (2\pi\sigma_\varepsilon^2)^{-\frac{1}{2}} e^{-\frac{z^2}{2\sigma_\varepsilon^2}} dz\right]$$

$$+ \sum_{\substack{\text{Obs in} \\ \text{Block 2}}} -\frac{1}{2}\ln(2\pi\sigma_\varepsilon^2) - \frac{(y-X_2\beta)'(y-X_2\beta)}{2\sigma_\varepsilon^2} + \sum_{\substack{\text{Obs at} \\ \text{Kink 2}}} \ln\left[\int_{\text{Kink 2}-X_2\beta}^{\text{Kink 2}-X_3\beta} (2\pi\sigma_\varepsilon^2)^{-\frac{1}{2}} e^{-\frac{z^2}{2\sigma_\varepsilon^2}} dz\right]$$

$$+ \sum_{\substack{\text{Obs in} \\ \text{Block 3}}} -\frac{1}{2}\ln(2\pi\sigma_\varepsilon^2) - \frac{(y-X_3\beta)'(y-X_3\beta)}{2\sigma_\varepsilon^2} + \sum_{\substack{\text{Obs at} \\ \text{Kink 3}}} \ln\left[\int_{\text{Kink 3}-X_3\beta}^{\text{Kink 3}-X_4\beta} (2\pi\sigma_\varepsilon^2)^{-\frac{1}{2}} e^{-\frac{z^2}{2\sigma_\varepsilon^2}} dz\right]$$

$$+ \sum_{\substack{\text{Obs in} \\ \text{Block 4}}} -\frac{1}{2}\ln(2\pi\sigma_\varepsilon^2) - \frac{(y-X_4\beta)'(y-X_4\beta)}{2\sigma_\varepsilon^2}. \tag{D.1}$$

ERROR PERCEPTION MODEL

In the error perception model, we assume that we observe all of the characteristics relevant to the household's water use, but the household's observed use may differ from its intended use. This discrepancy may arise for a number of reasons, for example, because the household finds it difficult to monitor total use over the bimonthly billing period, or because it cannot control the behavior of individual household members.

Since observed use is not necessarily equal to intended use, we cannot associate observed use with any particular block price (in periods when there is more than one block). For each observation, the likelihood function must incorporate the possibility that intended use could have been in any block or at any kink in the rate structure, and that the error term could take on any value between $-\infty$ and $+\infty$, assuming that the error term is normally distributed. Equation D.2 shows the resulting likelihood functions, where the first term represents periods when a single-block rate structure was in effect, and the remaining terms represent periods when a four-block rate structure was in effect.

$$
\ln L = \sum_{\substack{\text{Obs before} \\ \text{July 1991}}} -\frac{1}{2}\ln\left(2\pi\sigma_\eta^2\right) - \frac{(y-X\beta)'(y-X\beta)}{2\sigma_\eta^2}
$$

$$
+ \sum_{\substack{\text{Obs after} \\ \text{June 1991}}} \ln\left\{ \left[\left(2\pi\sigma_\eta^2\right)^{-\frac{1}{2}} e^{-\frac{(y-X_1\beta)'(y-X_1\beta)}{2\sigma_\eta^2}} \right] \cdot \left[\int_{-\infty}^{\text{Kink}\,1-y} \left(2\pi\sigma_\eta^2\right)^{-\frac{1}{2}} e^{-\frac{z^2}{2\sigma_\eta^2}}\,dz \right] \right.
$$

$$
+ \left(2\pi\sigma_\eta^2\right)^{-\frac{1}{2}} e^{-\frac{(\text{Kink}\,1-y)'(\text{Kink}\,1-y)}{2\sigma_\eta^2}}
$$

$$
+ \left[\left(2\pi\sigma_\eta^2\right)^{-\frac{1}{2}} e^{-\frac{(y-X_2\beta)'(y-X_2\beta)}{2\sigma_\eta^2}} \right] \cdot \left[\int_{\text{Kink}\,1-y}^{\text{Kink}\,2-y} \left(2\pi\sigma_\eta^2\right)^{-\frac{1}{2}} e^{-\frac{z^2}{2\sigma_\eta^2}}\,dz \right]
$$

$$
+ \left(2\pi\sigma_\eta^2\right)^{-\frac{1}{2}} e^{-\frac{(\text{Kink}\,2-y)'(\text{Kink}\,2-y)}{2\sigma_\eta^2}}
$$

$$
+ \left[\left(2\pi\sigma_\eta^2\right)^{-\frac{1}{2}} e^{-\frac{(y-X_3\beta)'(y-X_3\beta)}{2\sigma_\eta^2}} \right] \cdot \left[\int_{\text{Kink}\,2-y}^{\text{Kink}\,3-y} \left(2\pi\sigma_\eta^2\right)^{-\frac{1}{2}} e^{-\frac{z^2}{2\sigma_\eta^2}}\,dz \right]
$$

$$
+ \left(2\pi\sigma_\eta^2\right)^{-\frac{1}{2}} e^{-\frac{(\text{Kink}\,3-y)'(\text{Kink}\,3-y)}{2\sigma_\eta^2}}
$$

$$
+ \left[\left(2\pi\sigma_\eta^2\right)^{-\frac{1}{2}} e^{-\frac{(y-X_4\beta)'(y-X_4\beta)}{2\sigma_\eta^2}} \right] \cdot \left. \left[\int_{\text{Kink}\,3-y}^{\infty} \left(2\pi\sigma_\eta^2\right)^{-\frac{1}{2}} e^{-\frac{z^2}{2\sigma_\eta^2}}\,dz \right] \right\} \tag{D.2}
$$

The first term inside the brackets (for periods when the increasing block rate structure was in effect) shows the probability that intended use was in the first block times the probability that the error term was in the appropriate range to generate observed water use.[2] The second term shows the probability that intended use was at the first kink, in

_____

[2] Given observed water use y and intended water use $X_i\beta$, the error term η must be in the appropriate range to get from the intended block to observed water use. The likelihood function assumes that this range of error terms will be symmetric around zero, depending on whether observed water use is higher or lower than intended water use. The normal distribution is symmetric around zero, but it is an approximation of the actual error distribution, because water use cannot be negative.

which case there is only one possible error term, equal to the difference between the first kink and observed water use. The remaining terms show the probabilities that intended use was in the remaining blocks or kinks. Since the limits of the integrals depend only on observed use and the location of the kinks (which are in increasing order), the estimated demand curve is not constrained to be downward-sloping.

TWO-ERROR MODEL

The two-error model combines the two sources of error that are addressed separately by the heterogeneous preferences model and the error perception model. It assumes that the econometrician cannot observe all of the relevant characteristics that determine household water use, and that households' observed consumption may differ from intended consumption because of difficulties in monitoring and controlling use by household members over the bimonthly billing period. Therefore, intended water use $X_i\beta + \varepsilon$ (where ε is the econometrician's error term from the heterogeneous preferences model) could be in any block of a multiple-block rate structure, given observed water use $X_i\beta + \varepsilon + \eta$ (where η is the household's error term from the error perception model). The likelihood function for the multiple-block rate structure therefore combines the probability that intended water use is at any block or kink in the rate structure with the probability that the household's error term is in the appropriate range to get from intended use to observed use.

The likelihood function for the two-error model is given by equation D.3, assuming that the error terms ε and η are normally distributed and independent of each other.[3] The first term in Equation D.3 represents periods during which a single-block rate structure was in effect, and the remaining terms represent periods during which a four-block rate structure was in effect. The first term inside the brackets

---

[3]Given these assumptions, the joint distribution of $\varepsilon + \eta$ and ε will also be normal, and it can be factored into a marginal probability density function (pdf) and a conditional pdf that are both normal. The conditional pdf will depend on the correlation coefficient, $\sigma_\varepsilon(\sigma_\varepsilon^2 + \sigma_\eta^2)^{-1/2}$. See Hewitt [1993], p. 85.

shows the probability that intended water use was in the first block, times the probability that the combined error terms were in the appropriate range to generate observed water use. The second term shows the probability that intended water use was at the first kink, given observed use. The remaining terms show the probabilities that intended use was at the remaining blocks and kinks in the rate structure. The integral bounds for the kink points require that $X_1\beta > X_2\beta > X_3\beta > X_4\beta$, i.e., that demand be downward-sloping over the observed price range, as was the case in the heterogeneous preferences model. This constraint was binding for the estimated coefficients presented in Section 5.

$$\ln L = \sum_{\substack{\text{Obs. before} \\ \text{July 1991}}} -\frac{1}{2}\ln\left[2\pi\left(\sigma_\varepsilon^2+\sigma_\eta^2\right)\right]-\frac{(y-X\beta)'(y-X\beta)}{2\left(\sigma_\varepsilon^2+\sigma_\eta^2\right)}$$

$$+\sum_{\substack{\text{Obs. after} \\ \text{June 1991}}}\ln\left\{\left[\left[2\pi\left(\sigma_\varepsilon^2+\sigma_\eta^2\right)\right]^{-\frac{1}{2}}e^{-\frac{(y-X_1\beta)'(y-X_1\beta)}{2\left(\sigma_\varepsilon^2+\sigma_\eta^2\right)}}\right]\cdot\left[\int_{-\infty}^{\text{Kink 1}-X_1\beta-\frac{\sigma_\varepsilon^2}{\sigma_\varepsilon^2+\sigma_\eta^2}(y-X_1\beta)}\left(2\pi\frac{\sigma_\varepsilon^2\sigma_\eta^2}{\sigma_\varepsilon^2+\sigma_\eta^2}\right)^{-\frac{1}{2}}e^{-\frac{z^2}{2\left(\frac{\sigma_\varepsilon^2\sigma_\eta^2}{\sigma_\varepsilon^2+\sigma_\eta^2}\right)}}dz\right]\right.$$

$$+\left[\left(2\pi\sigma_\eta^2\right)^{-\frac{1}{2}}e^{-\frac{(y-\text{Kink 1})'(y-\text{Kink 1})}{2\sigma_\eta^2}}\right]\cdot\left[\int_{\text{Kink 1}-X_1\beta}^{\text{Kink 1}-X_2\beta}\left(2\pi\sigma_\varepsilon^2\right)^{-\frac{1}{2}}e^{-\frac{z^2}{2\sigma_\varepsilon^2}}dz\right]$$

$$+\left[\left[2\pi\left(\sigma_\varepsilon^2+\sigma_\eta^2\right)\right]^{-\frac{1}{2}}e^{-\frac{(y-X_2\beta)'(y-X_2\beta)}{2\left(\sigma_\varepsilon^2+\sigma_\eta^2\right)}}\right]\cdot\left[\int_{\text{Kink 1}-X_2\beta-\frac{\sigma_\varepsilon^2}{\sigma_\varepsilon^2+\sigma_\eta^2}(y-X_2\beta)}^{\text{Kink 2}-X_2\beta-\frac{\sigma_\varepsilon^2}{\sigma_\varepsilon^2+\sigma_\eta^2}(y-X_2\beta)}\left(2\pi\frac{\sigma_\varepsilon^2\sigma_\eta^2}{\sigma_\varepsilon^2+\sigma_\eta^2}\right)^{-\frac{1}{2}}e^{-\frac{z^2}{2\left(\frac{\sigma_\varepsilon^2\sigma_\eta^2}{\sigma_\varepsilon^2+\sigma_\eta^2}\right)}}dz\right]$$

$$+\left[\left(2\pi\sigma_\eta^2\right)^{-\frac{1}{2}}e^{-\frac{(y-\text{Kink 2})'(y-\text{Kink 2})}{2\sigma_\eta^2}}\right]\cdot\left[\int_{\text{Kink 2}-X_2\beta}^{\text{Kink 2}-X_3\beta}\left(2\pi\sigma_\varepsilon^2\right)^{-\frac{1}{2}}e^{-\frac{z^2}{2\sigma_\varepsilon^2}}dz\right]$$

$$+\left[\left[2\pi\left(\sigma_\varepsilon^2+\sigma_\eta^2\right)\right]^{-\frac{1}{2}}e^{-\frac{(y-X_3\beta)'(y-X_3\beta)}{2\left(\sigma_\varepsilon^2+\sigma_\eta^2\right)}}\right]\cdot\left[\int_{\text{Kink 2}-X_3\beta-\frac{\sigma_\varepsilon^2}{\sigma_\varepsilon^2+\sigma_\eta^2}(y-X_3\beta)}^{\text{Kink 3}-X_3\beta-\frac{\sigma_\varepsilon^2}{\sigma_\varepsilon^2+\sigma_\eta^2}(y-X_3\beta)}\left(2\pi\frac{\sigma_\varepsilon^2\sigma_\eta^2}{\sigma_\varepsilon^2+\sigma_\eta^2}\right)^{-\frac{1}{2}}e^{-\frac{z^2}{2\left(\frac{\sigma_\varepsilon^2\sigma_\eta^2}{\sigma_\varepsilon^2+\sigma_\eta^2}\right)}}dz\right]$$

$$+\left[\left(2\pi\sigma_\eta^2\right)^{-\frac{1}{2}}e^{-\frac{(y-\text{Kink 3})'(y-\text{Kink 3})}{2\sigma_\eta^2}}\right]\cdot\left[\int_{\text{Kink 3}-X_3\beta}^{\text{Kink 3}-X_4\beta}\left(2\pi\sigma_\varepsilon^2\right)^{-\frac{1}{2}}e^{-\frac{z^2}{2\sigma_\varepsilon^2}}dz\right]$$

$$\left.+\left[\left[2\pi\left(\sigma_\varepsilon^2+\sigma_\eta^2\right)\right]^{-\frac{1}{2}}e^{-\frac{(y-X_4\beta)'(y-X_4\beta)}{2\left(\sigma_\varepsilon^2+\sigma_\eta^2\right)}}\right]\cdot\left[\int_{\text{Kink 3}-X_4\beta-\frac{\sigma_\varepsilon^2}{\sigma_\varepsilon^2+\sigma_\eta^2}(y-X_4\beta)}^{\infty}\left(2\pi\frac{\sigma_\varepsilon^2\sigma_\eta^2}{\sigma_\varepsilon^2+\sigma_\eta^2}\right)^{-\frac{1}{2}}e^{-\frac{z^2}{2\left(\frac{\sigma_\varepsilon^2\sigma_\eta^2}{\sigma_\varepsilon^2+\sigma_\eta^2}\right)}}dz\right]\right\}$$

(D.3)

REFERENCES

Barakat & Chamberlin, Inc. *The Value of Water Supply Reliability: Results of a Contingent Valuation Survey of Residential Customers,* Oakland, Calif., August 1994.

Billings, R.B., and D.E. Agthe. "Price Elasticities for Water: A Case of Increasing Block Rates," *Land Economics,* Vol. 56, No. 1 (February 1980), pp. 73-84.

Brown and Caldwell Consultants. *Water Demand Investigation and Forecast,* mimeo, prepared for Alameda County Water District, November 1992.

California Department of Finance, *California Statistical Abstract,* Sacramento, Calif., 1992 and 1993.

California Department of Water Resources. *California Water Plan Update,* Volume 1, Bulletin 160-93, Sacramento, Calif., October 1994.

_____. *The 1991 Drought Water Bank,* Sacramento, Calif., January 1992.

_____. *California's Continuing Drought 1987-1991,* Sacramento, Calif., December 1991.

Carson, R.T., and R.C. Mitchell. *Economic Value of Reliable Water Supplies for Residential Water Users in the State Water Project Service Area,* QED Research, Inc., Palo Alto, Calif., June 9, 1987.

Dixon, Lloyd S., and Larry L. Dale. *The Impact of Water Supply Reductions on San Joaquin Valley Agriculture,* RAND, DRU-892-EPA, Santa Monica, Calif., 1994.

Dixon, Lloyd S., Nancy Y. Moore, and Susan W. Schechter. *California's 1991 Drought Water Bank: Economic Impacts in the Selling Regions,* RAND, MR-301-CDWR/RC, Santa Monica, Calif., 1993.

Dziegielewski, Benedykt, Hari P. Garbharran, and John F. Langowski, Jr. *Lessons Learned from the California Drought (1987-1992)* (Carbondale, IL: Planning and Management Consultants, Ltd.), September 1993.

Dziegielewski, Benedykt, Dan Rodrigo, and Eva Opitz. *Commercial and Industrial Water Use in Southern California* (Carbondale, IL: Planning and Management Consultants, Ltd.), March 1990.

Gleick, Peter H., and Linda Nash. *The Societal and Environmental Costs of the Continuing California Drought* (Berkeley, Calif.: Pacific Institute for Studies in Development, Environment, and Security), July 1991.

Griffin, R.C., and C. Chang. "Pretest Analyses of Water Demand in Thirty Communities," *Water Resources Research,* Vol. 26, No. 10 (October 1990), pp. 2251-2255.

Hewitt, Julie A. *Watering Households: The Two-Error Discrete-Continuous Choice Model of Residential Water Demand,* Ph. D. dissertation, University of California at Berkeley, 1993.

Hewitt, Julie A., and W. Michael Hanemann. "A Discrete/Continuous Choice Approach to Residential Water Demand under Block Rate Pricing," *Land Economics,* Vol. 71, No. 2 (May 1995), pp. 173-192.

Howitt, Richard, Nancy Moore, and Rodney T. Smith. *A Retrospective on California's 1991 Emergency Drought Water Bank* (Sacramento, Calif.: California Department of Water Resources), March 1992.

Just, R.E., D.L. Hueth, and A. Schmitz, *Applied Welfare Economics and Public Policy* (Englewood Cliffs, New Jersey: Prentice-Hall, Inc.), 1982.

Martin, W.E., H.M. Ingram, N.K. Laney and A.H. Griffin. *Saving Water in a Desert City* (Washington, D.C.: Resources for the Future), 1984.

Metropolitan Water District of Southern California. *The Regional Urban Water Management Plan for the Metropolitan Water District of Southern California*, Los Angeles, Calif., November 1990.

Moore, Nancy Y., Ellen M. Pint, and Lloyd S. Dixon. *Assessment of the Economic Impacts of California's Drought on Urban Areas: A Research Agenda*, RAND, MR-251-CUWA/RC, Santa Monica, Calif., 1993.

Nash, Linda. *Environment and Drought in California 1987-1992: Impacts and Implications for Aquatic and Riparian Resources* (Oakland, Calif.: Pacific Institute for Studies in Development, Environment, and Security), July 1993.

Nieswiadomy, M.L., and D.J. Molina. "Comparing Residential Water Demand Estimates under Decreasing and Increasing Block Rates Using Household Data," *Land Economics,* Vol. 65, No. 3 (August 1989), pp. 280-289.

Northwest Economic Associates. *Economic Impacts of the 1991 California Drought on San Joaquin Valley and Related Industries*, Vancouver, Wash., March 16, 1992.

Sewell, W.R. Derrick, and Leonard Roueche. "Peak Load Pricing and Urban Water Management: A Case Study," *Natural Resources Journal*, Vol. 14 (July 1974), pp. 383-400.

Spectrum Economics, Inc., and Sycamore Associates. *The Costs of Water Shortages: Case Study of Santa Barbara,* draft report to the Metropolitan Water District of Southern California, Los Angeles, Calif., October 1991.

Wade, William W., Julie A. Hewitt, and Matthew T. Nussbaum. *Cost of Industrial Water Shortages* (San Francisco, Calif.: Spectrum Economics, Inc.), October 1991.